Getting Away

MAHLON C. MORLEY
923 Foulk Drive
Belle Plaine, KS 67013

Resources for directors of Christian camps and retreats

GETTING AWAY

Marjorie L. Sanders

BROADMAN PRESS
Nashville, Tennessee

© Copyright 1984 • Broadman Press
All rights reserved

4275-23

ISBN: 0-8054-7523-0

Dewey Decimal Classification: 796.54
Subject Headings: CAMPING // RETREATS

Library of Congress Catalog Card Number: 83-70214
Printed in the United States of America

Unless otherwise noted, Scripture quotations are taken from the King James Version of the Bible.
Scripture quotations marked RSV are taken from the Revised Standard Version of the Bible, copyrighted 1946, 1952, © 1971, 1973.

Library of Congress Cataloging in Publication Data

Sanders, Marjorie L., 1933-
  Getting away.

  Bibliography: p. 93
  1. Church camps.   2. Retreats for youth.   I. Title.
BV1650.S26 1984   259'.8   83-70214
ISBN 0-8054-7523-0 (pbk.)

The author of this book gratefully dedicates it to camp leaders like Elise McCaa, who expressed the love of God to campers and staffers alike. She further dedicates it to the staffers with whom she had the privilege of serving throughout her fifteen years as camp director. Not only has she gleaned from them many of the ideas herein contained; but the rich harvest of friendships continues to enrich her life.

Acknowledgments

As compiler of this book, I gratefully acknowledge my indebtedness to the following:

The fellow staffers with whom I have served through the years. They have co-labored in the ministry of Christian camping by giving their energy, their love, and their creativity. Many of their ideas are reflected in these pages.

Audrey Smoak Manning, former assistant camp director, who painstakingly edited and gave suggestions concerning the entire manuscript.

Dr. Montague McMillan, former English professor, who read the manuscript and gave constructive criticism.

Janie Brooke, who proofread and corrected the final copy.

Mrs. Noble Y. Beall, Mrs. Paul Taylor, Mary Theresa Francese, Bob Taylor, Mrs. Ruby Boatwright, Dr. Johnnie Spaulding, and other friends and family who read the manuscript and gave suggestions and encouragement.

Those who have promised to promote the book.

Betty Chong, the typist.

Dr. Paul Carlson, who taught me many of the psychological insights included and who read over and approved these.

Preface

The writing of this book has been the result of fifteen years as a camp director and many other years as a staffer and a camper. I have sought to write the kind of helps I wish had been available to me as an inexperienced camp director. Therefore, the book has been written in great detail.

I hope the experienced director can enrich his program with ideas that may be new to him. Perhaps even familiar material might challenge the experienced director to new approaches and insights.

I have not expected to present a book that can be used effectively without adaptation. Every reader brings to his camping opportunity his own unique personality and expertise. Whatever is used from these pages, or from other sources, must surely be fitted to the purposes and the camper needs the reader deems appropriate in his setting.

MARJORIE L. SANDERS

Contents

1
The Purpose and Atmosphere of Camp

When a camp program is planned, goals should be set. Is the purpose of the camp to make Christ real and convince those attending that Christian principles work better than materialistic principles? Is the purpose to teach handicapped children to cope more effectively with their handicaps? Are you seeking to help grieving persons vent their grief and prepare to adjust to the loss of a loved one?

Is your main goal to help people to have a rewarding experience of fellowship? Do you plan for nature lovers to learn about birds through going on bird walks and to gather knowledge by seeing films and by hearing experts lecture?

The program should be planned carefully to reach your goals. Personnel serving those who attend your camp should have the training necessary to see that the camp goals are met.

Most of my years of camping were at a Christian girls' camp—where the emphasis was on Christian missions. Leading conferences were missionaries, both those from many countries overseas and those who worked among the people of special need in the United States. There was a pastor each week to present truths from the Bible. Devotional periods and Bible study were conducted by college-age staffers. Staff members were Christians who would seek to live out their faith in the camp setting.

Our camping experience did not allow for rugged camping with sleeping outdoors and cooking outdoors. We had a centralized program with an organized structure. We packed into every week as much teaching and activity as was possible in about five days with 180-200 campers per week.

There is a place for a structured camp, but being too highly structured can lead to deadness. Unwillingness to acknowledge the short attention span of young people can result in an outburst of misbehavior. My experience has taught me that people may learn to think of God in totally wrong concepts if Christian camp is a series of meetings with somebody always preaching at those attending.

I believe a child can learn to love God better at a camp where he has lots of fun than he can at one dedicated to teaching what God says not to do. I believe a lot of laughter at a Christian camp has greater possibilities of revealing the true nature of God than meeting after meeting of long, drawn-out sermonizing.

If a camp is done in the name of Christ and I am bored, I may begin to see God as a bore. If such a camp is full of deadpan people who tell me everything I do is wrong, I see God as a killjoy. If such a camp helps me have wholesome fun, I can better feel God's goodness. If vespers is a time of interesting talks (not too long) about God's love and power available to me, I may begin to experience God as a God of love. If I feel loved by staff and missionaries, I can hear them better when they tell me of God's love.

Every camp has a certain atmosphere. Of course, the camp setting has its effect. If a camp is located in a hot climate, a place for swimming is more important than in the camp that is located in a cool, mountainous area. Being in a wooded area beside a lake tends to cause a camper to have a feeling of quiet and peacefulness. In areas where birdcalls are common and creatures of nature are often sighted, there is a sense of beauty and wonder not available to those attending a camp program at the downtown church.

I do not believe I have ever attended any worship service that was as inspiring as my camp experiences close to nature.

All of life belongs to God. He is the creator of beauty and goodness surrounding us everywhere. I have sat beside the lake and watched a beautiful redwing blackbird flit to and fro on a canoe in the early morning. The red and yellow stripe across his wings flashed in the sunlight, and I worshiped the God who created him. While checking the camp at night, I have heard the whippoorwill calling. I have seen a rabbit stir in the pines. I have looked into a full moon. I have lifted my face to a host of twinkling stars and thought of the vastness of the mind of God. Only his wisdom could create millions of galaxies.

Standing on a hillside one afternoon, I heard the happy shouts of young people competing in sports events, and I thanked God for their health. I praised him for a free country in which to conduct a Christian camp.

One afternoon I was working in the chapel, preparing for a candlelight service that evening. The bell rang for swim time. A rush of laughing, squealing campers headed down the hill to the lake. I thanked God for the plunge into water that would refresh them on a hot day. While watching a water show, I saw campers dive off in beautiful form. I thanked God for their skill and coordination.

The setting for your camp may be the ocean, the mountains, or a cottage on the lake. Such settings have their own special beauties to offer. A program planned for the downtown church must rely on thought-provoking program material, varied activities, and enriching interaction with others and with God. The beauties of nature will not add the dimension available in an outdoor setting. Lovely interest centers, slides, or other visuals can, however, help to create atmosphere. The use of beautiful music also creates a desire to worship or sets a certain mood for many people.

The atmosphere of camp that meant most to me as a camper was a feeling of acceptance and caring. I am not sure how old my twin sister Margaret and I were when we attended a YMCA camp for underprivileged children. We were probably thirteen or fourteen. The one experience that stands out in my memory is that two staff members promised to come to see us when camp was over. They would be attending Converse College in our hometown. I do not believe we actually thought they would, but they did. That seemed a special expression of caring that we valued.

My first year as a camper at the camp I later directed was a happy experience. I was a teenager who made many new friends. We stayed awake at night giggling. The counselor kept telling us we would not get an honor award if we did not settle down. Somehow, the award just was not as important to us as our fun times at night. Even though I caused my counselor trouble, I still remember that I felt she cared for me.

The fellowship with others my age began relationships that continued through correspondence. One of these friends who wrote and had also laughed herself out of a camper award later married a minister. When I was camp director, her husband often served as camp pastor.

One reason I have given much space to the psychology of interaction and how to choose proper staff is that camp has everything to do with people relating to people. If I want to present Christ to you, I will do it by who I am and whether my relationships with you express concern.

I can remember the burden felt by staff members under my leadership who wanted children to love Christ. Sometimes they were deeply hurt by the spiritual insensitivity of these young people. I recall how concerned we all were over a camper we discovered was slipping off and getting "high" on drugs. We counseled with her, prayed for her, and corresponded with her.

Other children talked about the chaotic conditions at home caused by alcoholic parents. They wanted to know how to help these parents and how to live out their faith among relatives to whom God was mostly a name they used when swearing. Much evidence was shared with us about pressures felt by youth to drink, smoke, take drugs, participate in sexual experiences, and make fun of others. They asked for our prayers and support. In one week the emotional drain on a caring staff was enormous. Week after week our prayer was that such caring would encourage the campers to live for Christ and to continue to seek his help through prayer and the church.

2
Prayer in Camp Programming

Surely nothing could be more important in the life of a Christian camp than prayer. The Bible says, "Again I say unto you, That if two of you shall agree on earth as touching any thing that they shall ask, it shall be done for them of my Father which is in heaven. For where two or three are gathered together in my name, there am I in the midst of them" (Matt. 18:19-20).

To create a sense of the awareness of God, the staff needs to live close to him through prayer. I tried to create a schedule that interfered as little as possible with staff members' having a quiet time of prayer and Bible study the first thing in the morning.

I found myself anxious to get up ahead of the camp activity to be alone with God. Anything that interrupted my quiet time ruffled me. So I got up early and went out close to the beauties of nature or to the prayer room in our chapel. No other demands were upon me from any person.

I lifted each staff member to God. I asked God to speak that day through our guest missionaries and pastor. I prayed that campers would be spiritually sensitive. Burdens about special staff problems were often poured out to God. I sought his wisdom, his energy, his love.

I knew the staffers were often tired. So we had morning watch by rotating groups. The missionaries, pastor, and I spoke to the groups. At times we did have plays presented by the staffers, sometimes with camper assistance. However, this would usually not involve any staffer in more than one presentation a week. So, while campers attended morning watch, staffers were *urged* to use this time for their own devotions.

When it came to my attention that some staff member was abusing this time, I was firm in reprimanding him. It was easy to become careless and finish dressing during morning watch. I felt strongly, though, that any staffer who became careless about his own devotional life would soon have problems giving proper spiritual guidance to campers.

In order to unite the staff, I sought to teach them to pray together. No better means of developing a family spirit was ever invented. Of course, our staff members were varied in temperament. There were occasional personality clashes. We all felt irritated with each other at times. Just praying over our differences certainly did not resolve all differences, but it did help us to focus on God and his power to help. It helped us reaffirm our key purpose of serving campers who needed to know God better.

I remember a time when our staff members were supposed to conduct a Sunday morning worship service in a church about sixty miles away. The program had been planned. Several staffers had prepared talks. We had rehearsed our music.

But I had the distinct feeling that we were not in any spirit to be used as a blessing. I called the staff together in the chapel. We talked a while about the dead feeling among us. I was not the only one who felt it. Others were also concerned.

I urged that we pray more honestly to God than we had previously done as a staff. I do not remember who prayed that first courageously honest prayer, but it began to tear down the wall between God and us. I remember that a staffer then prayed something like this: "God, I don't like some things I see in several other staffers. Help me with my attitude. Speak to any of us who need to make changes in our lives."

The Spirit of God moved among us. I could feel him very real and renewing. When the last person spoke aloud to God, we sat silently. The service on Sunday was a powerfully lifting service of joy and praise.

Not only the staffers, but also the campers, need to learn to pray. It was enriching to visit in the cabins at night for devotional time. The counselor, or someone whom he invited, presented a spiritual meditation or story to campers after they were dressed for bed. Prayer time usually followed.

Often any campers who wished to pray out loud did so. One night I heard a camper pray, "God, bless the counselors, the lifeguards, the missionaries, the magicians. . . ." I wondered. We could use magicians at camp, but I did not know we had any. Then it dawned on me that we had listed in the program "musicians."

Types of Prayer

I believe prayer can become more meaningful if different types of prayer are used.

1. *Conversational Prayer*: This type of praying has been introduced by Rosalind Rinker in some of her books such as *Prayer: Conversing with God*. To pray conversationally is to copy the way we sit around our living rooms and talk to each other. For example, if someone brings up a topic such as inflation, everybody who has something to say on that subject talks about it then. They do not usually wait until we have moved on and are now discussing styles in clothes.

To pray conversationally means that a group of people bow their heads to concentrate on praying out loud. One person begins by bringing up only one subject. For example, the staff members may be praying at staff meeting as follows:

Staffer 1 may begin to pray out loud: "God, move among our campers this week. They seem so indifferent to spiritual things."

At that point, unless he has more to say on this subject, he pauses so others can pray on the same matter. Staffer 2 may pray: "Yes, Lord, our campers need you. They are loud and restless. I need patience in dealing with them. Help me."

Staffer 3 may pray: "Oh, God, there are two campers in my cabin who especially bug me. They make fun of everybody. They act as if they feel superior to others. I don't love them. But, Father, let me open myself so you can love them through me. Help me to want to love them, to care as you want me to care."

Conversational prayer is different from sentence praying. In sentence praying people usually pray only once and may pray a long time on a variety of topics. It can be difficult for others listening to focus their minds over a prolonged period of time. In conversational praying prayers should be brief and not wander from the topic. However, the same person may pray as many times as he wishes.

Perhaps staffer 3 has touched on a matter that causes staffer 1 to reenter by praying: "Yes, Lord, I,

too, have one problem camper who is of special concern. He is always by himself. I try to make him feel at home. I have attempted to get him talking with others in the cabin, but he just withdraws. Give us wisdom in dealing with him. Help the other campers to care enough to include him. Help him in his loneliness, O God."

In conversational prayer we can support each other. For example, staffer 2 may now pray, "O Lord, please do help this lonely camper!"

Everybody who wishes to pray about the campers and their needs will do so now. Then there should be a pause. A person may bring up a second topic. Staffer 4 may be tired and bored with camp, so he could pray: "God, I'm physically tired. I seem to be dragging, and it seems I've lost my enthusiasm. Energize me. Renew us as a staff. I feel a sense of boredom among us. We've been here for seven weeks, Father, and we need greater purpose. We seem to have lost it."

Staffer 3: "Yes, Father, I, too, am tired, and I find myself being irritable with the children. I realize they have come for fun and to learn. Help us not to cheat them."

The topic can change to as many subjects as there is time for, but someone may be designated to close. This can be especially needful if the time is limited.

2. *Praying by the Use of Litany*: A litany can be of just one type or can have several types divided into sections. An example of a litany of praise would be as follows (again, the setting for this will be the staff meeting at a camp):

Staffer 1: We open our lives to you, God, with wonder as we consider your wisdom. The vastness of your mind is beyond our understanding.

All: Praise be to thee, O God!

Staffer 2: God, we thank you for being a God of love. We praise you for sending Jesus to die for us. Such love is greater than our love.

All: Praise be to thee, O God!

Staffer 3: God, you are holy. The righteousness of your character is greater than our righteousness. You purify and lift us out of our lust, our selfishness, and our dishonesty. Keep on lifting us in righteousness.

All: Praise be to thee, O God!

Staffer 4: Lord God, thank you for being powerful. We are weak and helpless. You are mighty and able to help us in our weakness. Thank you.

All: We praise thee, O God!

In a litany we specify the type of praying to be done. We rehearse the one line everybody says together aloud. It is understood that this line is said in unison when each pray-er pauses. A litany can have a section of praise, intercession, thanksgiving, and forgiveness. The group can discuss ahead of time things they want to ask God for in intercession, special things they want to thank God for, and requests for forgiveness.

Litanies of praise should focus on the character of God. This is a time to become aware of who he is and his presence with us as we pray. Characteristics of God we listed in our litany are: wisdom, love, righteousness, power. Besides these, the group praying may list others, such as: forgiveness, patience, kindness, omnipresence, faithfulness. Members of the group getting into this type of praying can search the Scriptures between prayer sessions for new characteristics of God.

Intercessory praying in litany form could go something like this (again done by staffers):

Staffer 1: Lord, I want to ask you to give me new insight about how to teach the Bible study. Our campers seem disinterested. We cannot get them to open up. Help us know how to reach them.

All: We beseech thee, O God!

Staffer 2: God, you know how worried I am about my relationship with my girl friend. Her letters are few and far between. The times we have been together this summer have not been satisfying. Father, help me with my fear of losing her. Help me to release the situation to you and allow you to lead me.

All: We beseech thee, O God!

Staffer 1: God, I'm beginning to wonder if I should break up with my fiancée. I had thought she was the one I should marry until I came to this camp. Now that I've drawn closer to you, my fiancée and I seem so different. I've become committed to you in a way that she isn't. Give me wisdom.

All: We beseech thee, O God!

Staffer 3: Father, you know how angry I feel at my sister right now. I see her as a controlling person. I resent her. My feelings about her are hindering my ministry here at camp. Help me to release these feelings to you and allow your Holy Spirit to fill me.

All: We beseech thee, O God!

Staffer 4: I pray, God, that you will help me to overcome my feelings of pride. There are times when I glory in my own powers and ignore your leadership. Help me to be more humble and to give you the praise for the gifts you've given me.

Prayers of *thanksgiving* in litany form can go something like this (again staffers):

Staffer 1: Thank you, Father, for the sense of purpose I feel here at camp. Thank you for my health and for the happiness I experience playing and working here.

All: Thank you, O Father!

Staffer 2: Thank you that I received the scholarship I need for school in the fall. Thank you for the happy time we had last night in cabin devotions. I felt we were all so close to you and blessed by a sense of your love.

All: Thank you, O Father!

Staffer 3: Thank you that I have been able to forgive the staffer here I felt hurt toward. Thank you, God, that you led us to talk in such a way that understanding came. Thank you that it was your spirit that broke down the wall of misunderstanding. Bless all of us as a staff that our sense of pulling together may increase.

All: Thank you, O Father!

Staffer 4: Thank you, God, that John was able to accept you as his Savior as we talked last night. Thank you for the prayers of fellow staffers that helped him hear you speaking.

All: Thank you, O Father!

Prayers *seeking forgiveness* in litany might sound like this (again staffers):

Staffer 1: Dear God, forgive me for being impatient with the campers in my cabin today during rest period. Forgive me for having an indifferent attitude toward some of their needs. I find myself put out with them because they are noisy. Forgive any attitude in me that is contributing to the problem.

All: We beseech thee, O God!

Staffer 2: Lord, forgive me for being critical. Lately I have felt a great urging to talk about fellow staffers. This comes out of my own insecurity and unhappiness. Please forgive me. Help me to find what I need to secure me. Give me ways of finding joy. Help me.

All: We beseech thee, O God!

Staffer 3: Forgive me, Lord, for being hateful to a camper in my cabin whom I find obnoxious. Forgive my anger with him. Help me to care as you care. Give me wisdom in dealing with him.

All: We beseech thee, O God!

Staffer 4: Forgive me for not seeking your leadership in my life. Lord, you know that I have been running my own life. I have not asked you how you want me to use my talents. I have not sought your leadership in my relationships. Lord, you know my girl friend is not a Christian. I feel I love her. I have just left you out in this entire matter. I have not been wise in the way I could have with your direction. Forgive me.

All: We beseech thee, O God!

3. *Praying in Concert*: To pray in concert means that every person prays out loud at the same time. Some people find this type of praying difficult to get

into, but it is common among Christians in the Orient. Hearing all the voices calling on God helps me become more aware of his presence. It increases my sense of intensity as I pray.

This type of praying can be helpful when time is limited. It also can add a variety that lifts us out of a rut.

Usually, one person should be designated to close the praying with a loud "in the name of Christ. Amen."

4. *Praying Conversationally by Prayer Partners While Walking*: When the weather is nice, and the surroundings put persons close to nature, this can be a refreshing way to pray. People are asked to divide into prayer partners of two or three. These two or three people begin to walk together. Rather than talking to each other, they talk conversationally to God.

When people participate in this type of praying, they use the same model as I described in conversational prayer. In the use of this type of prayer, it is important to have enough room so participants will not interrupt each other. It is helpful to stress before the prayer time begins that everyone on the campsite needs to be in the proper spirit and continue praying until a bell is rung.

At our camp a staff member said she heard an interesting reaction after I explained the walking prayer. A camper asked, "Do we have to close our eyes?"

Prayer is the door through which weak, failing, burdened, anxious, and sorrowing human beings come face to face with the mightiest power in all the world. There is no weakness he cannot strengthen; no failure he cannot use as material for a greater success; no anxiety he cannot calm; no sorrow he cannot soothe.

Prayer is the bridge from grateful, joyous hearts to the great, glad Heart of Creation. Are we too busy to tell him our joys? Can he not make these richer? We who have no time to go to him with overflowing hearts, full of praise and awe, have no right to cross his bridge with our burdens and our woes. We who run our little lives without his help until our cables of success break down have no right to bring him broken cables to mend. Thank God that he is merciful enough to take us at our point of need, despite our unworthiness, and to mold us in his likeness. He invites us to come, no matter what our condition, and welcomes us when we do.

How many tangles we could avoid if we let him move the needle with which we weave our frustrated patterns. He, the Master Weaver, holds before him the pattern of what each life should be. Can he not direct better than those who cannot see the pattern?

Why are we not given the pattern? Because we would lose all if we failed to lean on him who is love and wisdom. If the Master Weaver gave us the pattern of what our life should be, we would likely run ahead of him and fall flat on our faces. Trusting him and listening for his guidance can lead to power and control. Christ in us is our only hope for wise living. Therefore, let us pray often.

3
Bible Study in Camp

Any Bible study conducted at camp will be more effective if the following conditions prevail:

1. You have no more than twenty-five children or youth meeting together.

2. You have two staff members working together to share ideas and bring more variety to the teaching.

3. The Bible study does not last over thirty to thirty-five minutes for small children through twelve years and not more than thirty-five to forty-five minutes for thirteen-year-olds and up.

4. No session is heavy with lecture. There needs to be a variety of methods including much participation by the campers.

5. If the same Bible study is taught a number of times during the summer, the teachers should vary the approach to teaching, lest they become bored. Plans for teaching, from day to day, should be revised through consultation if methods employed or preparation planned do not seem appropriate to the group. Be flexible. Try something else if the response of campers is sluggish or indifferent.

6. Let the campers talk enough that you will know where they live emotionally, spiritually, and socially, so that you can address their needs.

7. I have included in the Bible study material a variety of methods for approaching children and youth. The role play of the parable of the sower as I have described it will not go over with teenagers. It is designed for children six years to twelve years. Young children need guidance for doing role play, but they often enjoy doing this. Role play for teenagers can also be appropriate. A book on role play that gives much helpful information is *Value Exploration Through Role Playing* by Robert C. Hawley. This book was published by Hart Publishing Company, Inc., New York, NY 10012, copyright 1974. These are the topics covered: Decisions: An Open-Chair Role Play, Formats, Teaching with Role Playing, What to Do When Things Go Wrong, and Role Playing and the Development of Moral Judgment.

8. Any teacher needs material that includes lots of personal examples from real life to make Bible study relevant. I have included material that makes a point. I hope that teachers of the material will be stimulated to think of many other examples from their lives and the lives of people they know. To put a study across, teachers must personalize it.

9. Never choose a Bible study and expect to use it exactly as it is. We usually need to adjust, adapt, and add to such material for it to be suitable.

10. Create an atmosphere that will be appropriate for the study. If campers are physically uncomfortable, it will be difficult for them to concentrate. Those attending such a class generally need to sit in a circle. The teachers need eye contact with the campers to keep their attention. Anyone talking, whether camper or teacher, must be heard clearly, or all is lost.

It is important to realize that every person sits there in his own individual world. Unless you reach out and command his attention, he will continue an inner communication and dreaming that means he's tuned out. Call on him. Find out what his world involves. Maybe he is picking at another camper.

Several campers may be more interested in their communication with each other than they are with your study. *You* must involve them in the study. Change pace in what you do. Do a role play, then a quiz; then tell an example and have a camper read a few Bible verses that connect the thoughts. Divide them into groups and make a collage. Have a meditation time during which you play a musical record. Use posters, charts, and diagrams. Summarize the key thought at the end of each session. Vary the prayer experiences that accompany Bible study. (See the

17

section entitled Prayer in Camp Programming.)

11. Perhaps you are saying to yourself that nobody can put variety into a thirty-five-minute study. However, you can. The key to success is being organized so you shift smoothly from one activity to another. You will learn, by experience, what you can complete within a certain time limit. Constant adjustments in this type of planning should be anticipated. If campers respond better to one part than you expected, spend more time on it. Do not be rigid.

12. Campers need to bring a Bible to a Christian camp and use it in Bible study. But such use should be at brief intervals. As a young person, I remember being turned off by Bible study. Teachers had us go down the row and read verse after verse of Scripture. I could not keep my mind on such reading. I wanted to hear it explained and applied to my world.

13. Do not allow any camper to disrupt the study or to take over. Sometimes this may involve one teacher taking a camper outside for a talk while the other one continues with the study. Sometimes one young person gets attention by answering every question asked. You need to say, "John, I'm glad you know the answer, but I want some others to show me what they are thinking." If one person shares one long, drawn-out story after another, you will need to interrupt him as tactfully as you can and call on others to answer. There will usually be some shy campers who need encouragement before they will participate. The teacher needs to give this.

14. When you share personal experiences, tell your failures, temptations, struggles, and dreams. Do not paint yourself as such a saint that the campers cannot identify with you. Certainly you should feel free to tell ways you have been blessed by God and have experienced his victory; but if that is all you tell, a sense of unreality may well dominate the atmosphere. Participation may be slack.

15. A class that is conducted by teachers mostly in the Adult personality state will be far more productive than those conducted by the Critical Parent personality. The Critical Parent may react to confessions and different views with such comments as these:

"That's awful! You ought to be ashamed!"

"That was a dumb thing to do!"

"Well, that certainly would not honor the Lord!"

"You've got to be kidding! I've never heard of anybody doing a thing like that!"

"Are you ever out of it!"

"Honey, that must have crushed your parents!"

"I'm sorry to hear young people talk like that!"

"Remember, the Lord watches all we do!" (Said in such a way as to control through guilt.)

Of course, we are teaching Christian principles. I am not advocating not doing this; but if we want youth to share honestly, we need to withhold judgment and put-downs.

In the Adult personality we are calm, factual, thought provoking, able to treat others with respect, and desirous of allowing them room to express differing points of view. If we comment in a judgmental manner, the campers will not change their views. What they will likely do is keep their views to themselves.

The Adult will make comments or raise questions like the following:

"How old were you when this happened?"

"How did you arrive at that decision?"

"Were you pleased with the way this situation worked out? When faced with a similar situation in the future, how do you plan to handle the matter?"

"What other choices do you have?"

"What do you plan to do about this problem?"

"Where will you get money for that?"

"How old would you like your child to be before she/he begins dating?"

"How do you other campers feel about this problem?"

The clarifying response can sometimes encourage people to talk more. Example from a camper and teacher response:

Camper: "One time everybody in my crowd was making fun of a student at school. She wasn't dressed nicely, and her hair was cut funny. I know this was wrong, but I joined right in and laughed, too."

Teacher: "It sounds as if you felt torn between doing what you felt was right and fear of the group."

Camper: "Yes, I felt they wouldn't like me if I didn't do what they were doing. I wanted to speak to the girl, but I never did."

Teacher: "It sounds like you felt for the girl in her hurt and rejection, but allowed yourself a callous response out of fear of rejection by your group."

Camper: "Yes, that's right."

Teacher: "I appreciate the sharing of this personal struggle. Do any others of you have reactions or suggestions?"

(See characteristic 2—humble and gentle, within the Bible study chap. 5.)

The clarifying response stresses the feelings the teacher hears. Many times the person speaking has never cleared for himself exactly what feelings he is experiencing. No judgment needs to be made about the person's feelings. Feelings need to be *clarified* and *accepted.* The person can then explore the options he has of how to express these feelings.

Example of Critical Parent (or judgmental) reactions that have a tendency to inhibit participation:

Camper: "A 'so-called' friend of mine, Joe, has been going around the school telling lies on me. He talks like I will do anything a boy wants me to do. He says I've done things with him I haven't done. Man, I got so tired of it that I got him back good. A boy in my homeroom, Tom, had his bicycle stolen. I started telling everybody that Joe stole it. I said I saw Joe riding the bike in my neighborhood. Tom jumped on Joe after school one day and beat him up. I had one more good laugh off of that!"

Teacher: "Aren't you ashamed of yourself? Don't you know the Bible teaches us to forgive?"

Camper: "I'd like to forgive him, but several boys at school have called me ugly names. It is all because of Joe's lies. He got what he deserves."

Teacher: "The Bible says that we should let God judge others. It tells us we will be judged by God in exactly the same way as we judge others. You had better believe you stand under God's judgment right this very minute! You'll be sorry!" (This may stifle discussion and lead to a lecture and prayer.)

(See characteristic 6—forgiveness discussed within the Bible study chap. 5.)

Again, look at an example of the clarifying response:

Camper: "My mother makes me so mad! She nags me all the time. Sweep the kitchen! Empty the garbage! Wash the clothes! I will be looking at some interesting program on TV when she yells at me to run to the store for her. If I ask her to wait until the program is over, she gets even more bent out of shape. I finally do what she says to shut her up."

Teacher: "You sometimes feel that your mother is not considerate of you."

Camper: "That's right. She doesn't ever seem to feel anything I do is important. Whatever she wants done is the only important thing!"

Teacher: "You and your mother place a different value on things, and you feel she is unfair about how she treats you?"

Camper: "Yes, I do."

Teacher: "You sound *very* angry!"

Camper: "I am."

Teacher: "Is there any way any of you feel this situation could be improved?"

(Discussion)

Bible study that follows contains an emphasis on expressing our anger. You could have the camper discussing her mother to do a role play. She could first play herself. She could ask another camper to be her mother and tell the girl how to act.

Set up a scene similar to the one reported during the discussion. Then have the camper who is upset with her mother to reverse roles, to be her mother. The camper who played her mother becomes her. They enact the same scene. This may lead to insight into the mother's side of the problem.

Any incident involving anger could be similarly role-played as a part of the study.

Another way of helping the angry camper consider her mother's side would be to ask a rather mature camper to be the mother. She could be told lots about the mother: how many children in the family and any special problems they pose, the husband and the general condition of the marriage, the financial condition of the family, personality of the mother, whether she works and what she does. Then the camper (or a staffer if necessary) can sit in a chair and think aloud. She can talk about her anxieties, doubts, and any good feelings she has.

At the close of this soliloquy (talk to oneself), have a discussion.

4
A Bible Study: Growing in Christian Discipleship

Session 1
I Cannot Grow Without the Proper Foundation

It is certainly not possible to grow as a Christian until a personal experience has created a new awareness of need for change. When a genuine confrontation takes place between a person and Christ, there will be changes. We read, "Ye shall know them by their fruits" (Matt. 7:16a). Nicky Cruz, the young man who belonged to a gang in New York and had laughed when he saw blood, said he saw immediate results of his encounter with Christ. Formerly, little children ran from him. Now, as he walked down the sidewalk, some young children came up and began talking to him. They saw and felt the change. Can people tell that you are a Christian? How are you growing in Christian faith and practice?

Read Matthew 13:1-9,18-23 in several versions of the Bible.

Collect magazines ahead of time. Assign two groups of the campers the task of looking for pictures to make posters on these two topics:

1. Things that cause people to drift away from Christ.

2. What are some fruits of the Christian life?

While these campers are making posters, select nine or ten campers to act out the parable and its explanation in Matthew 13:1-9,18-23. Select one camper to be the narrator and read from *The Living Bible* or the Revised Standard Version, and campers act out the parable as interpretation.

Outline of Parable of the Seed

I. First Rendition of Parable
   A. Seed fell along path and birds devoured it.
   B. Seed fell on rocky ground and sun scorched it.
   C. Seed fell upon thorns and they choked it.
   D. Seed fell on good soil and bore again.

II. Second Rendition of Parable
   A. Hears and does not understand; devil snatches away—seed along path.
   B. Hears and receives with joy but in face of persecution falls away—seed on rocky ground.
   C. Hears Word, but cares of world and delights of riches choke it—seed among thorns.
   D. Hears and bears much fruit because he understands—seed on good soil.

III. People Needed to Role-Play First Rendition of Play
   A. Sower with a basket or bucket scattering seed (or a good substitute for seed).
   B. Two campers to be birds and flutter down to get the first seeds.
   C. Have some rocks over to one side and have sower scatter seeds there. Let one child wear a big sign around his neck with SUN on it. Have him squat down behind the rocks and rise up as narrator says the sun scorches seed.
   D. Have some thorn bushes in one corner of room and have sower scatter some seeds there. Also, have two campers with signs around necks that say THORNS. As seeds are thrown among thorn bushes, have campers reach down and act out "choking" motions.
   E. Have some regular soil in a cardboard box lid in the middle of the floor. Around this have several campers kneeling down on all fours. As sower throws seeds on them and the soil, have them rise slowly and stretch both arms upward.

IV. Role-Play Second Rendition of Parable
   A. Sower sows near a child busy reading. He

puts fingers in one ear and springs up and follows the sower. He then runs into a child with a sign around his neck, DEVIL. The devil acts out trying to persuade him against the sower. The child goes back and again sits down with his book.

B. Sower sows near a child who immediately jumps up smiling, laughing, excited. Two campers standing to the side come to him and pretend to be smoking. They offer him a cigarette. He refuses. They laugh and make fun. He then gives in to them and begins smoking.

C. Sower throws seed near another camper who follows him until several people on the sidelines stand up and offer him money, jewelry, clothes, or a tennis racket. He takes all these and goes in opposite direction from sower.

D. Sower scatters seed near a camper who follows him across the room. He gets his Bible and begins to witness to a camper watching the program. In the meantime, one camper has gone to a bunk and begins to moan. The new disciple goes to him, touches his head, and tries to comfort him. They bow their heads to pray together.

Conclusion: As soon as the role play is prepared, have the posters shown and explained by those who made them.

Session 2
Fruits of the Christian

Read Ephesians 4:1-32.

In Ephesians we are told of certain characteristics or qualities we will grow into if we are Christians:

1. *Loving—patient with others.* Certain people bug all of us. Who bugs you? Young people who always try to outdo you—do they bug you? Do you know somebody who brags on the trip he made, the grades he gets, and always seems to be trying to outdo you? Is there true competition involved here, or are you insecure and just think he is trying to outdo you? Maybe the person talking merely wants to share and make contact with you. Maybe he feels insecure and brags, hoping you will not notice the many faults he is overly aware of in himself. Psychologists tell us that the things we most criticize in others are those qualities we see in others that we hate in ourselves. List some things you dislike in others. Are you fighting any of these same weaknesses in yourself? How do you feel about you? The Bible says, "Love thy neighbor as thyself" (Matt. 19:19). It is a fact that we cannot love others until we love ourselves.

2. *Humble and gentle.* If I am humble, this does not mean I never stand up for myself. Being gentle with others involves trying to sense how others feel. If we can imagine how it feels to be alone in a nursing home, we can approach a grouchy elderly patient with more gentleness and understanding. Our own hurts and pains can make us more helpful to others who suffer. Charles Colson can minister to those in prison because he has been in prison himself. He was a powerful, selfish person working with President Nixon until he was convicted of crimes in relation to Watergate. He went to prison after he had a Christian conversion. From self-seeking to ministry, Charles Colson became an instrument in God's hands. Are you living in a home that is unhappy because of alcohol, fighting, or unfaithful parents? God can use your pain for your growth and ministry. Kneel down each night and ask his help.

3. *Being led by the Holy Spirit.* Christ used the time before he died to prepare his disciples for the coming of his Spirit. They found it hard to understand. At Pentecost three thousand persons were saved because this powerful Holy Spirit was poured out. God is a God of love. We can know this if we see Jesus as the best and clearest picture of what God is truly like. Nothing is true of God, so far as his basic nature, unless it is also true of Jesus.

Therefore, if we are willing to be led by the Holy Spirit, we will be led to goodness and love. Jesus said, "I am come that they might have life, and that they might have it more abundantly" (John 10:10). The Holy Spirit wants to lead us into this rich, full life Jesus talked about.

Name some things that the Spirit has led you to do. What is keeping you from knowing his leadership?

Catherine Marshall says in her book *The Helper* that a young woman named Doris had been sick. She was in a prayer group Catherine belonged to at the time. Another member of the group had a strong urging from the Spirit that all the group should place her in the midst of the group and pray over her. The group member who felt the urging to do this was not sure Doris would be responsive. She welcomed it. The group prayed for her. She was opened up and poured out the hurt of being sexually abused by her stepfather. All the pain of not being able to relate well to her husband and general fear of men came out. Doris was freed in such a glorious way that Catherine says she felt she was to be physically healed. However, she died shortly after the experience. But the peace of his Spirit's leading was a blessing to Doris and all the group.

4. *Our special gifts.* How blessed we are that we have all been given talents that can be dedicated to God and used to make the world a better place!

Corrie ten Boom grew up in a Christian home. Through her years as a prisoner of the Nazis, she was greatly strengthened. She then became a world traveler, sharing her experiences of God's goodness amid great suffering. She wrote books, one of which became a movie. Her gifts did not appear to be great, but she dedicated them to God and he enlarged them.

Dr. Paul Tournier is a famous Swiss psychiatrist. Obviously, his mental abilities are unusual. In one of his many books, Dr. Tournier tells of driving out to the edge of the woods. Leaving his wife in the car, he walked down into the woods alone. He knelt down and told God he wanted to give himself over completely to him. Dr. Tournier says that from that time his life changed drastically. He began to have a greater sense of purpose and fulfillment. In his counseling Dr. Tournier does not hesitate to point his counselees to God. He talks of listening to the needs and problems of one sitting before him. As they talk, Dr. Tournier says he prays for God's Spirit to move through him and through the counselee, to give wisdom and help. He does not believe his knowledge and experience are sufficient.

Whatever talent you have, give it to God. Great or small, he will enlarge and enrich it.

5. *Get rid of anger.* Anger is a common emotion to all humans. Anger, within itself, is not evil. When we feel angry, we need to acknowledge to ourselves what we feel. Then we can choose how we will express our anger. Assertiveness Training has become a popular way of teaching people to stand up for themselves in appropriate ways. According to this behavioral theory, there are two inappropriate ways of relating to others and dealing with our emotions that usually lead to worse problems. One of these is nonassertive behavior. If I am nonassertive, I hold my feelings in and am dishonest. If you do something I do not like, I smile and convince myself it does not matter. Turning my anger in on myself leads to depression. One definition of depression is anger turned inward on self. Emotions must go somewhere. If I hold my emotions inside, they can cause ulcers, headaches, and other unhealthy manifestations. If I am nonassertive, some of the results of much of my behavior may be depression or illness.

Aggressive behavior is defined as the second inappropriate way of relating. If I am aggressive, I explode at you. I let out my emotions as an attack on you. Your response will probably be defensive. You will probably seek to retaliate because you will feel put down.

The appropriate response is labeled *assertive*. This is a direct, honest reporting of my feelings. It is important that I realize I have the right to my feelings, whatever they are. But I can choose a kind, assertive approach. This approach will involve respect for others and respect for myself. Many times anger toward others is based on misunderstanding. If my approach is assertive, I will report my feelings and be open for your response. This has better possibilities for leading to clarification than aggressive or nonassertive behavior.

When Paul urged us not to let the sun go down on our anger, I believe he was urging us to seek to clarify things between us and those toward whom we feel angry. Simply reporting our anger in a kind way does not assure us the other person will respond so the matter can be cleared and the relationship restored. But, if I honestly direct my anger where it belongs, without attacking, I will feel better. Such reporting has better possibilities for success if we assure the other person we care for him and then are careful to relate with respect for him and self.

6. *Forgive.* How difficult forgiveness is! Jesus tells us his willingness to forgive us is dependent upon our willingness to forgive others. If we do not forgive, we break down the very bridge over which we, too, must walk as we confess to God. Corrie ten Boom tells of speaking in a church in Germany after being released from a Nazi prison. She looked up and recognized a former Nazi guard whom she knew to be cruel. He extended his hand as he expressed appreciation for her message. Immediately, she was stunned, unable to forgive, unable to extend a hand of friendship. Silently she cried out to God. He forgave through her.

Forgiveness is not a human achievement. It needs to be an opening of self to God. Perhaps God needs to put us in touch with faults within us that we need to correct. As we confess these, we may be in a better frame of mind for acknowledging our mistakes and accepting others who have wronged us. We need to ask God to bring about the forgiveness within us.

Supplement to Session 2

1. Divide campers into two even-sized groups with six to sit in inner circle, six in outer circle, and the rest on border of group.
2. Put these words on separate pieces of paper per word or phrase:
   A. Loving—patient with others
   B. Humble and gentle
   C. Being led by Holy Spirit

D. Using our special talents or gifts to serve Christ

E. Getting rid of anger

F. Forgiveness

3. The inner circle will be made up of six persons. They sit in a circle. Each is given a piece of paper with the lists of characteristics from session 2. They are to discuss these out loud with each other, telling about people they know who display these characteristics. They should discuss why they think Paul urged the Ephesians to develop these. They could tell whether they believe they possess the quality on their paper—to what extent? How can such characteristics be developed, etc.?

4. The outer group of six people should sit right back of the inner group. They are a listening team. They are not to talk until the counselor calls time on the inner group. Then they can give feedback of agreement, disagreement, or additional ideas and opinions.

5. Any campers other than the twelve can be allowed to say whatever they want to at the end.

Session 3
Growing as Jesus Grew

Read Luke 2:40-52.

Developing a balanced life is important. I know a person who works all the time. She is very conscientious, but overwork has often made her tense and cross. On one occasion when her co-workers were planning a covered dish luncheon, she was invited. She said she had more things to do than to participate in a dinner. The imbalance in her life has created a bitterness that people avoid.

An apt description has been given by some psychologists. They say we all have a Child living inside of us, the Child we once were. This Child needs to be allowed out to play. A good example of letting the Child out to play may be when we take a pleasure trip, fly a kite, go swimming, or go fishing.

Boredom is something we all have to cope with at times. If you go to school, do homework, keep your room straight, and do not play for a long time, you may get bored or depressed. No matter what age people are, they need to allow time for "the Child inside to get out and play." This social side of us needs fellowship and recreation. The Gospels tell of Jesus visiting in the home of Martha, Mary, and Lazarus. We know he attended weddings.

A great deal has been said in recent years about heart attacks being related to lack of exercise and smoking. A recently developing treatment for cancer is nutrition. A doctor who wrote a book on breast cancer urges people to cut down on sugar and to add yeast, wheat germ, and various vitamins to their diet. He says the diet he proposes is proving effective.

The body throws off many cancerous cells. Only when it is unhealthy and weak can the cancer cells get a hold on the body. Dr. Carlton Fredericks says a buildup of sugar affects the body adversely in its fight to eliminate cancer cells.

Attention is being called by nutritionists to the additives in foods. When we read the labels on catsup, cereals, packaged cornbread, and canned fruits, we often see sugar listed as the second ingredient. This means there is only one other ingredient in larger quantity than sugar. Sugar and salt are acclaimed damaging to us in large amounts. Whole wheat breads are being recommended more highly than white because of their nutritional value.

Dr. William Glasser is a psychiatrist who came up with a theory he calls positive addiction. He contrasts it with negative addiction. Negative addictions are smoking, drinking alcoholic beverages, depending on drugs, and the like. The nicotine in cigarettes is highly addictive. People who start smoking find it very difficult to stop. But this addiction is negative because nicotine coats the lungs and causes emphysema and lung cancer and can contribute to heart problems. Alcohol and other drugs can become addictive to the point that a person completely loses control of himself. He may insist on getting doped up, even if this causes him to lose many jobs and finally lose his family. The person feels compelled to do drugs even though they are taking other pleasures and successes from him. Certainly this is a negative addiction.

Dr. Glasser describes a positive addiction as something you develop a compulsion to do. You feel pain or guilt when you do not do it. It gives pleasure and builds up the person who becomes addicted. Jogging is one addiction many Americans are finding beneficial. Dr. Glasser interviewed and questioned joggers who said they jogged so regularly that they felt guilt (or pain) when they missed. Joggers who became positively addicted found their minds spinning out, experienced creative insight into problems, felt their worries drift off, and returned home renewed and relaxed.

Christians need positive addictions, not negative ones. The Bible tells us our bodies are the "temple of the Holy Spirit" (1 Cor. 6:19, RSV) and that we should keep them clean for his indwelling. Mental development can enrich our usefulness and our personal vitality. Dr. Viktor Frankl was a prisoner of the Nazis for many months. He discovered that those who endured the degrading and cruel treatment of their captors were more often mentally strong than physically robust. A sense of hope and meaning in the life of a prisoner could keep him going when hunger plagued him and physical exhaustion was overwhelming.

We need to read healthful, wholesome books. We need some close friends whose faith inspires us. Services of worship can lift us beyond ourselves to God. Keeping busy with visiting the lonely and needy can strengthen our thoughts and purpose more than a constant dose of TV. We need times when we look at and listen to lots of beauty. As a counselor, I hear many sad and ugly stories. Some of them are about the neglect of parents, alcohol and drug abuse, defeat and despair. At a time when I felt depleted, I realized I needed to absorb more beauty to offset the ugly. I went to a garden concert and tour, took a trip to the mountains, and attended the ice follies. My mind was renewed.

The Bible tells us that Jesus increased in wisdom. I do not believe we can honor God with ignorance. As a summer missionary in St. Louis, Missouri, I had to listen to a minister who had no training. He made no advance sermon preparation. Wherever the Bible fell open, he started reading. He preached whatever popped into his head. It was bad. In fact, it was embarrassing.

Learning can be an exciting adventure. There is a dead quality about people who learn something and keep depending on the same narrow bit of knowledge year after year. They begin to think and talk in ruts. They become a bore.

I believe God's call to us usually brings with it a time of preparation. Jesus was taught at the Jewish Temple, and the Gospels tell us nothing about him from age twelve until he began his ministry at about thirty. Perhaps this was because he was spending much time in study, prayer, and preparation before he began his ministry. This means that most of what we read that Jesus said and did took place in three years. His work had quality because it was preceded by thorough preparation. "Study to shew thyself approved unto God, a workman that needeth not to be ashamed" (2 Tim. 2:15).

Spiritual development is essential to wholeness. The spiritual has to do with the inner life, the soul, the spirit in us that never dies. Webster defines spirit: "the breath of life: the animating or vital principle giving life to physical organisms . . . a supernatural, incorporeal, rational being or personality usually invisible to human beings but having the power to become visible at will . . . the active essence of the Deity serving as an invisible and life-giving or inspiring power in motion . . . one manifestation of the divine nature . . . the activating or essential principle of something influencing a person."

How can the moral, inner, religious nature be developed?

1. Our spirit is renewed through fellowship with other persons who see life from a spiritual viewpoint. My Sunday School class has taken an interest in a prisoner, John, who used to be one of my students. He has become a Christian, and the transformation in his life is evident. On two recent occasions members of my Sunday School class have gone with me to visit John. He says we have encouraged him. By the same token, his faith has also encouraged us.

The last time a member and I visited John, the prison visiting area was crowded. Two prisoners sat against the wall near us and could probably hear everything we said. As we prepared to leave, I asked John if he wished us to pray aloud or to pray silently for him as we traveled home. He said, "I'm not ashamed. Let's pray aloud." We did.

One summer as we began summer school, I felt depleted. Among the students was a lovely girl in a wheelchair named Jeanette. I asked Jeanette if she would be my prayer partner, and she agreed.

We would meet together in my office and read a few verses of Scripture. We talked out our needs and prayed aloud. Jeanette was simple and refreshing in her approach. She did not word her prayers to impress anybody. She talked to God as to a good friend.

Gradually, the tired, bored feelings I felt began to lift. Hearing Jeanette pray for me was encouraging.

At the present time Jeanette is married and lives in the same town I do. Once when we talked, she referred to the good memories she had of the summer we prayed together.

Ed will readily tell you he is a born-again Christian. He was suspended from our school a number of times but returned this year on a work scholarship. He said that recently a staff member stopped him in the hall and commented on the change she has seen in him. "You are keeping a low profile and not causing any trouble," she said. He replied, "When Christ takes over, he makes changes in people."

I suggested to Ed that we pray together about once a week. Our first time of praying together occurred while he rode with me to run an errand. As we approached Easter, Ed told me how he had been thinking of what Jesus suffered for us. We talked about the problem Jesus had breathing while hanging on the cross, the heat of the day, the scourging before he was crucified. On Easter, as I worshiped in my large, formal home church, I thought of Ed and rejoiced in his newfound faith. I also rejoiced that our fellowship was renewing my faith.

2. Spiritual growth calls for reading the Bible and books of faith, attending services of worship, and praying alone and with others. In *Guideposts* magazine a young woman has told of learning to meditate and gain power spiritually. Her father was a doctor who worked from 7 AM to sometimes 7 or 8 PM. At noon each day he came home and went into a quiet room alone for thirty minutes. Once she asked him what he did during that time. He said he stilled and quieted himself until he was in touch with the Infinite. She saw the power this gave him. She set out to find a similar power, which she has written into a book to be published soon. Her father told her that each person must find his own path to getting into touch with God. How true!

Yet it is easy to neglect the spiritual simply by running the TV all the time, gossiping with friends instead of praying with a needy friend, or staying busy with projects that make no room for listening to God. Jesus prayed all night before selecting his disciples. It was his practice to go to the Temple. He rose long before day to be alone and pray, we are told. He was in an agony of prayer before he faced the cross. He prayed for those who crucified him. He told Peter, "I have prayed for you" (Luke 22:32). He knew how weak Peter was and how he was to be tempted. Of course, we remember Peter denying Jesus when he was arrested. In Philippians we read, "Have no anxiety about anything, but in everything by prayer and supplications with thanksgiving let your requests be made known to God. And the peace of God, which passes all understanding, will keep your hearts and your minds in Christ Jesus" (Phil. 4:6-7, RSV).

Balance is the key word for Christians! We need to grow spiritually, socially, mentally, physically. When we lack balance, there is uneasiness, irritation, a lack of vitality.

Supplement to Session 3
How-Healthy-Are-You Test

I. Physically
  A. Do you exercise twenty to thirty minutes three to five times a week by walking, swimming, jogging, or biking?
  B. Do you eat:
    1. Green leafy vegetables several times a week?
    2. Some fruit every day?
    3. Cereal that has little or no sugar?
    4. Whole wheat bread at least three times a week?
    5. Milk once a day?
    6. No more than one dessert a day?
  C. A minimum of eight hours of sleep almost every night?

II. Mentally
  A. Do you read or listen to the news two or three times a week?
  B. Do you read a book every three months?
  C. Do you belong to any clubs or develop hobbies that teach you new things? (Missions organizations, bird watching, stamp collecting, etc.)
  D. Do you study for school at least three afternoons or nights a week?

III. Spiritually
  A. Do you read your Bible at least three days a week?
  B. Do you attend Sunday School almost every Sunday?
  C. Do you attend missions organizations or Church Training most weeks?
  D. Do you participate in or encourage family devotions?
  E. Have you visited a sick person or ministered to someone in need within the last two weeks?
  F. Do you pray every day?

IV. Socially
  A. Have you made a new friend in the last year?
  B. Have you invited someone to visit you or to go somewhere with you in the last two weeks?
  C. Have you tried some new activity in the last year? (Like bowling, skiing, tennis, or learning to play an instrument you have been willing to play in front of others?)
  D. Have you attended a play, recital, reception, wedding, party, athletic event, or other social occasion within the last month?

Scoring: Each question you answer yes gives you one point.
22 is a perfect score
18-21 is excellent
15-17 is good
10-14 is fair
0-9 Get to work!

Session 4
Growing a Great Faith

Read Matthew 13:31-33; Mark 4:31-32.

Do the Value Sheet on Faith and discuss it. (See Supplement to Session 4, no. 1.)

One reason John, the prisoner I mentioned earlier, is growing a great faith is that he is being tested every day. Some months ago he had roommates who ridiculed him every time he read his Bible. They cursed God, and one of the men beat John so hard that he had to go to the hospital.

Earlier in John's life, he would have whined and felt sorry for himself. The change he has experienced, however, caused him to turn to God. He said God spoke to him in his pain to remind him of ways he has hurt others in the past. Such pain became redemptive for him.

Joanne, we will call her, attended our school about eight months to complete her high school work. She had inherited a rare and crippling disease. Her life had been filled with many situations over which she had very little control. This had created much anger which was gradually expressed as we had counseling sessions.

Joanne had met a fine young man, Bill, who had the same disease she had. His father was a minister, now retired. Bill's family invited Joanne home with them for weekends and holidays. It was evident that Joanne was being enriched emotionally, socially, and spiritually by this Christian family.

Bill and Joanne were married, and the women of their Lutheran church gave the reception. Blue Cross-Blue Shield hired both Bill and Joanne, and they began a very important and happy phase of their lives.

When Joanne felt a lack of challenge in her job, she attended Midlands Technical College to complete the respiratory therapy course and worked one summer for a doctor.

This year Joanne is attending Columbia College. At Christmas Bill and Joanne visited me, and Joanne described the struggle she had had studying genetics. It had looked likely that Joanne might have to repeat the course. She put in hours of study to prepare for the exam.

As she entered the exam room, Joanne sat quietly and thanked God for helping her learn all she had. She asked him to help her be calm and recall the information. As she opened the exam, she laughed aloud over all she knew. The professor graded her paper before she left, and she made ninety-one.

Joanne's faith has grown through the influence of a Christian family, through her own ventures, and through hard work. She loves and trusts God more the longer I know her.

A man who had been paralyzed during the war lay in bed, bitter and discouraged. He gained an insight into how positive mental pictures can lead to a miraculous change in behavior. He began to meditate and hold in his mind pictures of standing, walking, running. Over long months of doing this, he struggled through painful therapy. At long last, he was able to walk and run again. Of course, there are cases of paralysis that such meditating might never help; but there is power over our behavior that begins with the pictures we hold in our minds.

If we picture ourselves as odd and left out, we begin to act this way. If we picture ourselves as defeated losers, that is what we become.

A lady came to Dr. John A. Redhead, a minister. She was to make a speech and she was petrified. Dr. Redhead told her to spend time each day picturing herself giving the speech. She must drive out any pictures of fumbling and blunders. Rather, she must picture herself calm, doing well, with an audience responding positively. She gave a successful speech.

Read Hebrews 11:1 and discuss. Catherine Marshall recommends keeping a log of specific requests of God and notes on when and how God answered.

Supplement to Session 4, No. 1
Value Sheet on Faith
(For Session 4)

1. A man complained in Sunday School that he did not receive a pay bonus. He said others who had been there the same number of years he had were receiving a bonus. It was suggested by the Sunday School members that this might be an oversight. He was asked if he had checked into the matter by consulting the boss, or the proper employee. He replied, "If God means for me to have more money, he will take care of it." What is your response to this?

A. I agree. _____
B. I have doubts about this being the best response. _____
C. I consider this a totally ridiculous way to respond. _____

2. A man was having pains around his heart. He refused to go to the doctor. He said that God is the Great Physician and asked all his family and friends to pray for him.

A. I agree that he did the right thing. _____
B. I strongly disagree. _____

C. I consider medical help and prayer the best combination. _____

3. A neighbor was having trouble sleeping at night. She has a son who is known to be an alcoholic. He goes off on drinking sprees and is sometimes unable to work for three weeks. When neighbors were discussing how helpful it is to discuss personal problems with a counselor, she said, "I just take my problems to God. I don't believe in depending on other humans."

A. I agree. _____
B. I strongly disagree. _____
C. I think she is partly right. _____

4. A man has made a commitment to Christ. He has told God he wants to be all that God wants him to be. He is a chain smoker. When a Christian friend talked to him about the victory he had with overcoming smoking, he concluded by saying, "And if you had enough faith, you could stop, too." What is your reaction?

A. I agree. _____
B. I think it takes more than faith. _____
C. I think the Christian friend is being too judgmental and piling up guilt. _____

5. A friend has been a church member for many years. She gave a testimony during a special service at the church and told of being baptized by the Holy Spirit. She later began sharing with members of the church how she can speak in tongues. She left her husband because of problems they had for many years. She has not worked regularly. She talks a lot about God providing and meeting her needs; relatives often give her money to help her. What do you think of her baptism of the Spirit?

A. Sounds great! _____
B. Her life sounds mixed up. _____
C. I do not believe God is the one leading her to be lazy and expecting others to meet her needs. _____

6. John and Mary have been dating for two years. They are both sixteen. They had a fuss recently and both feel they have been wronged. Mary calls her best friend about meeting to pray. They pray and ask God to help Mary and John see themselves properly and move in their lives so they can come to an understanding. Mary calls John to tell him she wants to get together and see if they can work things out. They do. What part did faith play in this problem?

A. None. They worked it out themselves. _____
B. Praying helped Mary have a better attitude, but I do not believe it actually affected John. _____
C. I believe the Holy Spirit helped Mary gain a better attitude and prepared John's heart for reconciliation. _____

Supplement to Session 4, No. 2
Value Sheet on Faith
(for Children)

1. You are having a test in school tomorrow. You know you need to study. You also want to attend a church meeting. You go to church and come home so tired you can only study thirty minutes. You ask God to help you make a good grade on the test.

A. Since God wants you to attend church meetings, he will see to it that you do make a good grade on the test. _____
B. God expects you to study all along and arrange your time so you can attend church and study. _____
C. God will help you think of answers, even when you do not know the material, if you are surrendered to him. _____

2. Some friends you are with begin to make fun of a girl who does not dress and act as they do. You join in. Later you feel bad about this. You pray and ask God to forgive you.

A. You believe God does forgive you, even though you continue to ignore the girl. _____
B. You ask God to forgive you, and you take time to chat with this lonely girl a little. _____
C. You talk to several of your friends one at a time about how you feel that the girl needs kindness. You express your concern for her. _____

3. You have accepted a part in a play about a missionary to be presented at evening worship service. You have attended many rehearsals. You have studied your part and said it out loud in front of a mirror at home. You know it but are nervous. You ask God to help you remember your lines. Do you think God will honor such a prayer?

A. Yes _____
B. Maybe _____
C. It depends on how nervous you are. _____
D. You should not bother God with such little matters. _____

4. You get into lots of fights with your brothers and sisters. You keep asking God to help you be good. Why do you keep fussing when you do not want to?

A. You do not have enough faith, or you could stop. _____
B. Growing emotionally is a slow process. Some fussing is only normal. _____
C. You could talk to one or both parents, and ask them to help you and your brothers and sisters

figure out ways to have less conflict. (Example: Take turns with chores and choosing TV programs. This might involve having a family council meeting.) ———

D. God wants to help you. Family devotional times might help. ———

E. God does not expect you to overcome such problems overnight. The answer to such a prayer may take time and growth. ———

5. You want to be a great Christian. You hear a missionary doctor speak. You tell God you are willing to go anywhere and be a missionary doctor and serve him. You make average grades. You never have liked science. Becoming a doctor means studying lots of science. You know God will make you succeed. God can do anything. You are excited about becoming a missionary!

A. God wants you to consider the talents and abilities you have. ———

B. If you have enough faith, you can do anything you want to do. ———

C. The greatest way for you to serve God may not be as a missionary doctor. ———

D. Time, other influences and interests, and development of abilities will give you direction later in life. ———

Supplement to Session 4, No. 3
I Am David Livingstone

I am David Livingstone and my life was a life of faith. In my home in Scotland, my parents and grandfather loved to share stories. One of my favorites was about a missionary doctor in China. This story made me dream of doing the same type of work.

When I was ten years old, I began working in a mill from 6 AM to 8 PM each day. I studied between my job of tying broken strings. I went to school at night. I was promoted to full spinner at the mill and saved enough money to go to Glasgow and study medicine.

Hearing Robert Moffat tell of seeing the smoke of a thousand villages in Africa where no missionary had ever been fired my imagination. The London Missionary Society agreed to send me as a doctor to minister to this dark continent. I began going from village to village healing the sick and helping build canals to hold rainwater, for this was a dry land. I started Sunday Schools and told stories about Jesus around the camp fire at night.

I hated the slave trade and fought it many years. In one village we tried to rid ourselves of some lions. I was attacked and my shoulder was never normal again. Malaria made me sick. I was often separated from my family and lonely. Only my faith in God kept me going.

My wife gave birth to our fourth child. Afterward, she took a fever and died. What a lonely feeling to have to leave my motherless children and continue to travel! But I had to share Christ and stop slavery. After traveling six months for over fifteen hundred miles, in fever, hunger, and danger, we found the coast. Now more missionaries can present Jesus, and better trading may help cut down slave traffic!

My followers found me dead on my knees in prayer. My spirit was now at rest with God. These loving followers took my heart and buried it under a tree near the village of Chitambo. My heart belonged to Africa. My body was embalmed, and my followers carried it thirteen hundred miles to the coast. My body was placed in Westminster Abbey in England, and my life continues to inspire the faith of those who hear.

5
The World of Children and Youth

If our camp programs are to provide the atmosphere for growth and inspiration we desire, we need to have some familiarity with the particular problems, interests, and goals of those who will attend camp.

I present here some general information concerning the consideration that should influence plans for children and youth.

Nine Through Twelve Years

In working with children nine through twelve years of age, we need to remember:

1. They are active and need much participation, both physical and mental. This means we need active, competitive sports. When we teach, we need to involve campers in role play, quizzes, puzzles, buzz groups, and poster making. They need diversified projects such as crafts, nature hikes, and swimming.

2. They are emerging from childhood during which their entire world has revolved around parents and home. They are now more interested in children their age, in belonging to clubs, in being active in choirs, and in sharing ideas with other children. Home is still important, but they are broadening their world.

3. Children nine through twelve are more interested in their own sex. This is the beginning of the "gang" age.

4. Most children of this age like to learn new things. They are impressionable and can be influenced to broaden their thinking. They have a basic sense of justice that can be altered or enlarged.

5. They can be taught the difference between right and wrong. This is an important time for instilling good moral principles. These can best be taught as they are applied to the typical world of play, school, and home.

6. Children of this age often look up to older youth. It is important that staff members at a Christian camp have basic Christian character and reflect proper attitudes. Children *will* be influenced by these people.

7. Children nine through twelve are at an age where many of them may be ready to make a public confession of their faith in Christ. It is important that they feel no pressure that tells them when they must make a decision. They need a clear presentation of how to be saved. They need a personal time with a staff member or pastor who can answer any questions and pray with them.

8. Emotionalism should be discouraged in dealing with children. Again, they will tend to be upset if others are upset. They need staff members who are even tempered and dependable.

9. Homesickness among this age group is rather common. They especially need to feel loved by their counselor. If a camper is frequently seen alone, the counselor needs to ask others to bring the camper with them to supper, include him when they go to crafts, and keep talking to him, even if there is little or no response. All staff members need to be aware of loners and to help with this problem.

Rainy days are a special challenge when you are trying to help a homesick camper get over the hump. I have included some ideas in this book that you could use on rainy days, especially the indoor fair. It is also nice to collect many indoor games. I attended a camping conference and learned about some fine wooden games I asked our board of trustees to begin buying for our camp. One or two were purchased each year. They lasted well. You can order a catalog for such games from: Worldwide Games, Box 450, Delaware, Ohio 43015. Included are: Dutch Shuffleboard, Korean Yoot, Chinese Friends, Shisima of Kenya, French Table Cricket (similar to football), English Skittles, American Marble Football, American Sockey, American Box Hockey, Bumper Puck, and others.

Thirteen Through Eighteen Years

Teenagers are facing a complex stage of growth. We need to keep these facts in mind as we work with them:

1. Teenagers are experiencing many physical changes that create moodiness. Young women are often influenced in what they feel like doing by their menstrual cycle. Most teenagers feel so insecure that they resort to some cutting down of others. They need understanding and emotional support. They need encouragement to participate, or they will choose to sit and become bored. Do not try to drag them into activities that are too threatening. They hate to be embarrassed and they can easily feel this way. Females spend a lot of time dressing and often feel they look terrible. They need honest affirmation. Young men may be self-conscious about a changing voice or the fact that they are skinny or fat. A period of awkwardness is common to teens, both male and female.

2. Teenagers are interested in the opposite sex and are sometimes insecure about reaching out. As a general rule, girls mature about two years ahead of boys. Therefore, girls are usually much more interested in boys than the boys are in them. This is frustrating. Teenagers do not need ridicule about their interest in the opposite sex. They need support in feeling that this is normal. They need guidance in the type of contacts they make and in rules that will help them feel secure about what is appropriate behavior-wise. When teens are given too much freedom, they feel unloved. Caring involves guidelines. Regret and fear can plague the teenager who has too much freedom.

3. Relationships with the same sex are also important to teens. Having a "best buddy" to do things with is important. Sharing activities in groups gives support and mutual give-and-take that teens usually enjoy. The "gang" becomes more important than parents. Often there is sharp conflict between parent rules and teen standards.

4. Teenagers are beginning a long process of seeking independence. Children nine through twelve may accept parents' beliefs and standards as theirs, but teens question everything. They want to do what the "crowd" does. They want more freedom. They often complain that parents treat them like babies. It is natural for the teenage period to be a stormy one in relation to conflicts with parents.

5. Teenagers tend toward periods of sluggishness, due to physical changes. They need time to day-dream. Most teens are involved with thoughts of the future: whom he will date, whether he will marry, what vocation he will choose, how many children he may have, where he will live, and what kind of person he will become. It is normal for teens to need time to listen to music and fantasize. Music is a big part of the world of most teens. Sometimes sports are equally important.

6. Getting a part-time job and making practical plans for the future become more and more important. Teens are faced with coming to know themselves, discovering what their talents and capacities are. They are faced with learning to make a living. They must decide whether to go to college or to work full time. Sometimes they are faced with the decision about marrying early. *Teenagers certainly do not respond well to being told what to do about anything.* Sometimes they can be challenged to think and question. We must look for the proper opening to reach them if we would seek to help them choose wisely. They need to face facts and reality and compare these to unrealistic dreaming.

7. This is a world very hung up on sex. Teenagers are pressured early to participate. They often know very little about the threat of VD. They may even be given the facts about various birth control methods and not be told how becoming pregnant can affect emotions or how an abortion leaves emotional scars on some people. Teenagers need to realize the financial and emotional strain of parenthood.

8. Teenagers can be reached with truth about God. They can be challenged to commit their lives to Christ. Putting their trust in someone who will lead them into the future and give them wisdom in making decisions can be stabilizing.

9. Teenagers need to be given room to question moral and religious issues. We do not need to deal with them in such a way that we give them "pat" answers. Let us ask questions that touch reality. Let us be honest about what we do not know. Let us admit that we are still searching.

6
Using Behavior Modification to Shape Behavior

An understanding of some counseling theories might be helpful in working with campers. One basic fact to remember is that every camper is seeking a place among others where he can receive recognition. Dr. Thomas A. Harris, author of the best-seller *I'm OK—You're OK*, has pointed out that basic needs include recognition. People not only need air, water, and food; they need attention. The spinal cord can shrivel up and people can lose weight, sleep, and even the will to live as a result of lack of human contact.

At camp it will be evident that campers are seeking attention. Some have learned to get positive attention, while others have learned to get negative attention. The positive attention getters will cooperate by cleaning cabins and by being quiet at night or during rest hour. They may excel in sports and treat other campers and staff members in a friendly way. The rewards of such action will be new friends, awards, a sense of acceptance, and goodwill.

The negative attention getters may refuse to make up their bunks or to attend certain meetings. They may make cutting remarks to campers and staffers, may destroy property, and may sneak off and smoke pot. In other words, they are setting themselves up to be kicked and put down. Actually, they may feel more comfortable with a negative reaction than a positive one. People tend to be comfortable with that which is familiar to them.

It is important not to reinforce a young person for doing negative things. For example, you may be having a devotional time with your campers. The camper who collects negative attention may begin all kinds of distractions. He may whistle, throw paper, or giggle. If you can ignore him, he will not receive his reinforcement. He is seeking attention. You give him the payoff he seeks if you call him down. In fact, he then has everybody's attention. If he is ignored often

enough, he may experience enough pain to change his behavior.

Withdrawal or time out from the group may also help. During Bible study, if you have a "clown" who gets lots of laughter from the group, calling him down only gives him more attention. Taking him to a room where he is completely away from the group has the possibility of withholding a payoff. This may gradually produce change.

When people are seeking attention in wrong ways, they need to be offered ways to receive positive attention. For example, if you discover your "troublemaker" or "clown" can sing well, ask him to sing a solo at vespers or at the talent show. If a person who provokes others and makes enemies is a good swimmer, maybe he can represent the cabin in swim competition. If he receives a blue ribbon and words of praise, maybe he can begin to see himself more positively. A camper who uses a string of ugly words may get his payoff if you as counselor act shocked. If you ignore him, perhaps he will drop such an outburst; but he needs another opportunity for getting attention. Maybe he can tell jokes well. If so, listen and respond. This will positively reinforce him.

Some laws of behavior modification that might be good to keep in mind are:

1. When an event or action is followed by a pleasing reward, it is more likely to occur again.

2. When an event or action is followed by punishment or unpleasantness, it is less likely to be repeated.

3. A reward must be given immediately after the action one wishes to reinforce in order for it to be associated clearly.

4. Whatever is chosen as a reward must be something of significance to the individual being rewarded. If it is to be *positive,* it must be something liked and

enjoyed. If it is to be a *punishment*, it must cause a sense of loss or pain to the person one is seeking to break from a certain action.

5. A person may participate in an activity he dislikes if it is paired with a reward he values. For example: If John does not like Bible study, but loves to swim, set up your schedule so he can go swimming after Bible study. If he misbehaves in or cuts Bible study, take away his swimming privilege.

Positive rewards at camp could be:

1. Praise
2. Ribbons, trophies, certificates, or other awards
3. Extra time in swimming or playing tennis
4. Being excused from cabin cleanup or kitchen detail
5. A role in a play, a part in a talent show, participation in sports contests
6. Extra candy, dessert, or other food that is liked
7. Excused from usual lights out. Extra time after lights out to do something enjoyable

Punishment at camp might include:

1. Extra cleanup duties
2. Going to bed earlier than usual
3. Having to do push-ups or extra physical exercise (Sometimes rowdy campers who are keeping counselors up until the wee hours every night can be helped to settle down by physically tiring activities that are extra.)
4. Cutting out canteen time or desserts
5. Withholding attention

Sometimes people try to set up the same rewards and punishments for everybody. This does not work as well as an individual system. What rewards one camper may have no significance for another. Being denied swim time for a camper who loves to swim is a significant loss that may cause him to alter his behavior. But for a camper who does not enjoy the water, withholding the swimming privilege is no loss at all. Learning the likes and dislikes of campers is necessary before an individual system of reward and punishment can be established.

The shorter period of time you work with a camper, the less possibility you will have of changing his behavior. Established patterns of getting attention can be very hard to change. Do not expect the impossible.

7
How Our Personality States Affect Relationships

Some years ago Dr. Eric Berne introduced a theory called Transactional Analysis. According to this theory, we have three personality states. These three states are Parent, Adult, and Child. The Parent personality is composed of a Critical Parent that nags, finds fault, and is very judgmental. A person in a Critical Parent state is usually emotional and may point a finger while preaching at or talking down to another person. The Critical Parent often makes others feel scared or angry. Being bossy with others has a way of hooking them into dependence or rebellion. If persons have grown up with too much Critical Parenting, they can develop strong not-OK feelings about themselves.

The Nurturing Parent personality state is a supportive, loving state. If a person comes to you upset and crying, you may hook into your Nurturing Parent personality and talk reassuringly, put your arm around the person, and help him to feel more valuable and less alone. A person who had parents who nurtured him a lot (acted out of the Nurturing Parent) usually likes himself. He may not get upset over his mistakes, especially if his parents treated mistakes as something we all make that can usually be corrected. We all need nurturing (care, support, encouragement, affirmation, love, physical affection). We will never outgrow these needs.

Developing a Parent personality state makes it possible for us to give guidance to others. Some parenting is needed from camp staffers to campers. Rules about behavior at camp—time to go to bed, required activities, ways people must treat each other, and rules of safety—all come from the Parent. These provide order for the camp. Overparenting can, however, cause resentment and squelch creativity. There needs to be time when campers have a choice about activities. There need to be opportunities for creative

contests, talent shows, and fun times that allow individuality. Overparenting by a strongly nurturing person can cause too much dependence. This can hook into the weak, inadequate feelings. What people need is support, but the kind that encourages them to use their resources. This fosters mutual respect.

A camp program that is planned purely by the Parent will be too heavy with meetings. It will involve "what is good for the child" kind of thinking. Structuring every minute will tend to be the order of the day if the Critical Parent is planning. In our Critical Parent we tend to need to be in control. When those planning camp have an overriding desire to be in control of everything that happens at camp, this can be oppressive. As I have said, when I first began planning and directing camps, I had too much control.

Dr. Berne says the brain works like a recorder. Everything we have ever experienced, including emotions, is recorded. Incidents in the present stir up old feelings from the past. Another way to say this is, the not-OK feelings in the Child personality get turned on by incidents in the present. These feelings can be the explanation for why a camper cries, becomes defensive, or begins to scream at someone. Seeing the situation ourselves, we may feel shocked. We would not expect such an outburst. The response seems too emotional for the small incident that seemed to trigger it.

Under such circumstances, the Nurturing Parent personality of the staffer in charge needs to be as calm as possible. It will probably be best to take the camper into another room and gently try to let her get out all her feelings. Let her tell what happened in the present and give her feelings. *Never tell her she ought not to feel that way!* We all have the right to our feelings, whatever they are. Being told we should not feel that way only adds guilt or anger. It does not help. To respond in this way would be to hook into the Critical Parent. This will only cause hurt and defensiveness. The Nurturing Parent can show understanding and patient acceptance.

The person handling this situation needs to *listen, listen, listen!* Then, in the Adult personality, he needs to concentrate on saying things that indicate he *hears* and is trying to understand, such as: "I can see that this has really upset you! This must be a painful experience. I'm sorry you feel hurt. I'm sorry you feel nobody likes you. *Have you ever felt this way before?* Has this same type of situation ever happened to you before? Tell me about it."

When we ask questions our Adult should ask the type that will get the most information rather than ones that can be answered with "yes" or "no." For example, "Tell me about it." Questions that can be answered with only one word can begin to sound like the Spanish Inquisition. You wind up pumping for answers rather than saying enough to allow them to pour out feelings naturally.

In the Adult personality state we are unemotional and logical. This is the personality state that looks at facts and raises lots of logical, rational questions such as: "If I do this, what will be the results?" Having a strong Adult state makes it possible to make better decisions.

If we were cut down as children, we did not learn to value ourselves properly. We need to reparent the not-OK Child living inside. This must be done through the Adult personality by learning to stand up properly for ourselves. When someone is cutting to us, the old not-OK feelings in the Child put there by the Critical Parent get all stirred up. The Adult needs to stand up and protect the Child in a healthy, firm, assertive way.

Another way the Adult can help reparent the Child is to seek nurturing where it is available. Many times people tend to keep going back to the people who belittle them. It is not possible to make friends with everybody. Therefore, spending as little time as possible with people who put us down can be a way of protecting the Child. We need all the affirmation and good feelings we can get. Making *friends* with people who are willing to nurture us is important.

We need a lot of planning and thinking before and during camp that come out of the Adult personality state. The Adult needs to make plans that set up a clear *contract* with every staff member concerning duties that must be performed, time off, salary, and what can be expected when staff members are out of

line in relation to rules and duties. Some type of staff book needs to be written and given to staffers to read. Then all rules and duties need to be discussed openly. Each staffer needs a clear understanding of where his duties end and someone else's duties begin.

The following is an example of a written contract to be signed ahead of camp:

Staff Contract

I agree to serve in the position of *Counselor* at Camp _____ for the following dates: _____. I realize that I will be *required* to attend training sessions the following dates: _____.

I realize that this is a Christian camp. Therefore, I will seek to reflect Christ in my behavior and teaching of campers. I will not smoke, drink alcoholic beverages, or take drugs of any kind.

In the position of counselor I agree to the following duties:

1. I will take care of welcoming new campers, helping them make a satisfactory adjustment. I will guide my cabin members concerning where they should be according to camp program. I will see to their safety and stay close to the cabin at night to keep them quiet and check on special needs. I will oversee quiet during rest period.

2. Bible study teaching will be a regular part of my duties. I will study and seek to make this effective.

3. I will conduct devotional periods in my cabin each night.

4. I will accept specific program duties, such as working with crafts, sports, drama, nature study, and the like.

5. I will attend regular staff meetings.

6. I will assist with dining hall cleanup.

7. I will assist campers in keeping up with their belongings and managing their money.

8. I will cooperate in any way I can to help the camp succeed.

_____ _____
(Signed)   (Date)

The camp promises to pay $_____ weekly for services rendered by *Counselor.* The camp promises regular time off. Lodging and meals will be furnished to all staffers by the camp.

_____ _____
(Signed by Director)   (Date)

We need the use of all our personality states. If we are logical, thinking, planning all the time, we are in our Adult almost constantly. This makes us a bore. We need to be able to play. To do this we must let out the Child personality. Being able to tease, laugh, and be warm and affectionate all depends on letting out the Child. We all know how easy it is for most children to hug people around the neck. Such warmth is easily lost in adulthood. But how essential that we be able to let out loving feelings toward others all our lives! This is the core of developing supportive relationships.

The Child state in each of us is composed of the feelings that developed in us from birth to approximately five years of age. The Parent and Adult regulate when we hook into the Child. The key consideration is appropriateness. If we act scared or laugh a lot when meeting with the board of trustees of our camp, this will be to our disadvantage. Being in our Adult will make us able to discuss matters calmly and logically. This will produce more respect.

Staffers who hook into the Child personality to perform skits or compete in the greased watermelon contest will delight campers.

A camp program planned by the Parent-Adult-Child can provide better balance. The Child is not only the center of feelings but the personality state we are in when we become creative and spontaneous. I once heard Dr. James Sullivan, at that time executive secretary of the Baptist Sunday School Board, tell the story of a little girl sitting with her mother toward evening. As they were watching the sunset, the mother said to her, "Hasn't God painted a beautiful sky for us this evening?"

"Yes," said the little girl, "And just to think, he did it with his left hand!"

"What do you mean? Why do you say that he painted it with his left hand?"

"Well he *had* to do it with his left hand. The Bible says Jesus is sitting on his right hand."

Children have fresh, new approaches to things. What they think and feel has a tendency to come out naturally. At camp we need fun times, some feeling times, some times to discover God's creation. This is not possible in an overly structured setting.

Awareness of whether others are relating to us out of Parent, Adult, or Child can allow us to choose the personality state we will hook into in response.

Here is an example of how to overcome conflict: Let us suppose that a staff member comes to you, upset about his duties. He feels you have given him too much to do. He will come on out of his Critical Parent and can sometimes hook into the not-OK feelings in your Child.

Staffer (Parent): I am so upset! You must think I'm Wonder Staffer! I simply cannot handle all the sports events and also set up this extra Olympic field event! You are being unfair!

If the staffer hooks the camp director's Child ego state, he will probably jump up into his Critical Parent and fight back.

Camp Director (Parent): Well, after all, everybody is busy. You don't have a cabin to see about twenty-four hours a day. You aren't on the waterfront four hours a day. I see no reason why you can't do what I've asked you to do.

The outcome of this will probably be anger and misunderstanding.

On the other hand, if the director will choose to act out of his Adult, he may be able to move the staffer into his Adult.

To the same upset comments by a staffer, the camp director might respond out of his Adult:

Camp Director (Adult): I'm sorry you feel such pressure. I'm sure I have given you a big job. Perhaps I was thoughtless in assigning too many duties to one staffer.

Staffer (Adult): Well, I do feel I just can't do it all alone.

Camp Director (Adult): Let's sit down and figure out what staffers might be moved from other duties to help you.

Staffer (Adult): OK.

Because the director stayed in his Adult, the staffer was pulled out of his Parent state into his Adult.

The transaction could then be diagrammed:

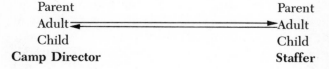

8
Breaking Up Psychological Games

One emphasis of the Transactional Analysis theory is that people sometimes play psychological games. These games are never played when people are in the Adult personality state. They are played when people are in the Child or Parent personality states. Such psychological games always involve a desired payoff and some hidden or covered message. These games involve dishonesty that tends to confuse relationships. There is always a psychological level underneath not in tune with the words being said. We learn to play such games in our homes. We are not aware of them unless someone points them out. We are only aware, usually, of predictable ways of relating.

People often resist efforts to break up such games because they are not familiar with other ways of structuring their time. Also, the games *do* get attention. They provide a way of becoming involved with people. What makes them unsatisfactory is that they confuse people and usually lead to bad feelings.

Let me describe some psychological games you may encounter at camp. Keep in mind that these games may possibly be broken up by your being in your Adult personality. Acting out of your Adult will mean you will be calm, logical, and unemotional. This will keep you from hooking into the game and giving the desired payoff. Not receiving the payoff may encourage the person to do some thinking through that can lead to giving up some of the games. In your Adult personality you will be able to act in such a way that you do not take responsibility for the other person. You will take responsibility for yourself and your actions.

No. 1 Game: Poor Me

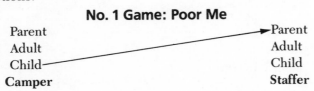

Camper: "Nobody likes me. I'm nice to everybody. But everybody ignores me. Why does everything always turn out this way? People don't like me at home. Everybody picks on me. I don't do anything to deserve such treatment. Poor me!"

(The camper is coming on like a Victim, wanting you to rescue him and feel sorry for him. If you do this, you encourage this dependence and his feeling sorry for himself. The thing you need to know is what he is doing that is creating this painful situation.)

There is some connection between people's behavior and how others are reacting to them. For example, a teenage girl was being made fun of by a group near me at lunchtime. I wondered why. Later, a friend brought her to me and said she needed to talk to me. She had fallen into the habit of letting guys do sexual things with her for the attention she got. She had only been at our school for a few days and had already allowed a boy to become very familiar with her. She talked about people making fun of her. She did not need my sympathy. She needed me to lead her to evaluate her situation and ask her what she was doing. Then I could point out how her lack of self-respect was teaching others to treat her with disrespect. She needed help in learning to value herself.

I think a Christian camp is an ideal place to help people recognize their worth. After all, we have all kinds of opportunities to teach that God loves them so much he sent his Son to die for them individually. Listening to them when they talk, respecting them, channeling their abilities, loving them, and seeking to understand them all communicate God's love.

No. 2 Game: Why Don't You . . . Yes, But . . .

The person who starts this game starts off by asking for advice. He hooks others into the Parent personality by coming on out of his Child. He presents a problem which others try to solve. What makes this a game is that the person presenting the problem does not actually want help. His goal is to defeat the Parent he calls forth.

Example:

Parent	Parent
Adult	Adult
Child	Child
Camper	**Staffer**

Camper: "My mother won't let me go anywhere but to church. It gets so boring at home."

Staffer: "Have you ever given her any reason to mistrust you? Is this why she only lets you go to church?"

Camper: "No, I always behave. She just doesn't trust me."

Staffer: "Are your friends at school the kind of friends your mother trusts?"

Camper: "Yeah. She likes them fine."

Staffer: "Do you bring them home with you so she can really get to know them?"

Camper: "Sure. Sue, Carolyn, and Dee Dee come home with me often. She lets us be at home together, but we can't go anywhere."

Staffer: "Are you saying your mother won't let you go to ball games, or to skate, or anywhere but church?"

Camper: "That's right."

Staffer: "Have you ever asked your mother to go with you skating, or to whatever event you wanted to attend?"

Camper: "Yes, but she always says she's too busy."

Staffer: "Well, I don't know what to suggest, then. I'm sorry."

This is now the time to give a sigh of defeat at failing to help. The camper gets the payoff then because she rendered a Parent figure impotent. Such a camper is probably growing up in a home where she is constantly told what to do by parents and maybe older brothers and sisters. Remember that her goal is not to get help but to defeat you. She is probably not being honest about some of her answers. Do not allow her to pile up guilt. Stay in your Adult, so the responsibility for this problem rests with her.

If you are hooked by a game one time, you can learn from it. Invariably, the person will play the same games over and over. Therefore, you can gradually learn how not to give the desired payoff if you wish to defeat such a game.

No. 3 Game: The Rescue Game

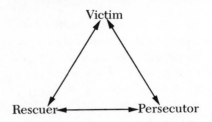

Many games actually fit into this triangle. Some person comes on as a poor, pitiful victim. Another person gets hooked into feeling sorry for him. Then someone plays Persecutor and punishes one person involved in the game.

The reason the arrows go in all directions is to indicate that people can quickly change from Victim to Persecutor, or from Rescuer to Victim, or from Persecutor to Victim.

Example: Suppose Camper #1 is always behind in making up his bed before inspection, so a friend, Camper #2, continually plays Rescuer and helps him. Camper #1 runs out of money for canteen, so Camper #2 gives him some of his. One day Camper #1 is chosen as captain of one softball team during recreation time. He knows Camper #2 loves to play ball, especially to be the pitcher.

Camper #2 keeps begging Camper #1 to choose him for his team, which he does only after he has chosen four other campers. Finally, after he is chosen and has asked if he can be pitcher, Camper #1 chooses someone else to pitch.

What do you think is going to happen? I say Camper #2 is going to switch from Rescuer to Persecutor.

Often we mean well when we rush in to help others, but we need to remember that *helping* in the right way involves hooking into the strength in the one we seek to help. He has power he is presently unaware of, but he can be plugged into it. Such an approach breeds respect, not I'm OK—you're not OK (superior-inferior relationships).

In his book *Scripts People Live*, Dr. Claude Steiner says we can know we rescued instead of helped if:

1. We did more than 50 percent of the work.

2. We wound up angry at the person we attempted to help.

No. 4 Game: Now I've Got You—You Dumb Bunny

In this game the player is trying to hook you into feeling bad about yourself. He probably has a low sense of his own worth. If he can hook you into making a mistake, he can feel superior to you temporarily.

For example, suppose the campers are trying to organize a skit. Camper #1 and Camper #2 have seemed to be leaders in the cabin. But Camper #1 leads by aggressive, manipulative means. He is easily threatened by people who have ability and a good self-image like Camper #2. Camper #1 knows the skit they are to do and has seen it presented. He has told it to Camper #2 but left out some parts (the sure way to pull off "Now I've Got You—You Dumb Bunny").

At this point Camper #1 and Camper #2 are explaining and demonstrating the skit to the other campers in the cabin.

Camper #2: "So, then, one of you will bend over and let the other camper jump over you."

Camper #1: "Are you kidding? That would never work, John! That would look stupid."

Camper #2: "But I thought that's what you wanted in order to give the idea of one being a rock and the other a frog jumping over it."

Camper #1: "No, we won't need any frogs or rocks, silly!"

Camper #2: "Oh, well, I'm sorry. I thought I understood, but I guess I didn't."

Camper #1 wins when Camper #2 apologizes and feels bad, especially if he's whiny and embarrassed.

No. 5 Game: Kick Me

This game is played by people who feel bad about themselves. The worse a person's self-image, the harder version of this he will play. The person playing this game does things to get others to put him down because he believes he deserves to be punished. He may feel he is basically a bad person because parents have emphasized his badness and punished him often.

An example of a person who plays "Kick Me" is the woman who marries an alcoholic who beats her. When he dies, she is likely to marry another alcoholic or someone who will punish her unless she has counseling.

Once a lady finally left her alcoholic husband she had run away from home to marry. She divorced him and married a kind and considerate man. All he did for her left her feeling so guilty and unworthy that she scrubbed all the floors every day as self-punishment. For a while after her hard work she would feel a sense of relief. Finally, she sought counseling. She discovered that it was her father's mistrust of her that led her to the conclusion she was a bad girl needing punishment. She gradually learned to value herself and to be able to accept her husband's kindness as something she deserved.

At our school there was a young man who was always sloven in appearance. He would not bathe. He said silly and antagonistic things to provoke people to cut him down or to laugh at him. He played "Kick Me" because the way he grew up somehow influenced him to feel he was worthless and deserved punishment.

An example of what might happen at camp is:

Camper #1 is silly when everyone else is serious for Bible study. The other campers call him "Silly" and tell him to hush, his payoff.

Give him an assignment for Bible study for the next day that will put him in a positive light. Compliment him on things you do appreciate about him.

Camper #2 runs on the pier at the waterfront. All campers were told from the first that this was against the rules. He is called down by the waterfront director in front of everybody at the lake. He feels bad. This is his payoff.

If the waterfront director can take the camper aside to correct him quietly, this might be better. Also, asking him to be in the water show or to help some camper perfect a new stroke can give positive attention.

No. 6 Game: Uproar

This psychological game involves a verbal fight. The payoff for it is a guilt-free separation on the part of the two players.

For example:

Parent   Parent
Adult   Adult
Child   Child
Counselor #1   **Counselor #2**

Counselor #1 (in Adult personality state): "Did you know the campers in your cabin are making lots of noise?"

Counselor #2 (The not-OK feelings in his Child personality are hooked, and he jumps into his Critical Parent personality): "Well, look at Perfect Counselor! Have you checked your cabin lately? The last time I passed by, they were making far more noise than mine."

Counselor #1 (now in his Critical Parent personality): "Well, my goodness! You don't have to be so defensive. I just wanted to make you aware of your cabin."

Counselor #2 (Critical Parent): "I would prefer that you mind your own business like I do. I didn't run and tell you about your cabin being noisy."

Counselor #1 (Critical Parent): "Well, I'm sorry I brought it up! I'm going out to the bathhouse to take a shower."

(Slams the cabin door as he leaves.)

The payoff comes with the separation. He may go visit another staffer and will probably be a while getting back. Sometimes people play this game under the pressure of being confined too long and too closely with certain people. Adequate time away from camp will probably cut down on this type of conflict.

If roommates have not been honest about the things that bug them about each other, they may unconsciously provoke a fight like the example just given. It is important to clarify what each roommate expects in a living situation. For example, if Counselor #1 has been borrowing Counselor #2's clothes, without permission, Counselor #2 may be angry. One comment about her campers being noisy could cause an angry response. The real issue might be the clothes.

No. 7 Game: If It Weren't for You

In this psychological game a person can always find somebody else to blame. He refuses to take responsibility for his own behavior.

Example: Tony, a counselor, has been called in by the camp director for leaving his cabin unattended at night.

Camp Director: "Tony, I have been concerned about your campers. I have been by checking cabins three nights this week, and you were away from the cabin."

Tony: "Well, I'm sorry, but I noticed other counselors who leave their cabins unattended."

Camp Director: "Tony, we are trying to deal with each staffer and see that he carries out his duties. Presently, we are talking only about you and your cabin. You are not responsible for how any other staffer functions. You can only control your behavior."

Tony: "I just know that I'm not the only one not doing his duty."

Camp Director: "Tony, just let me ask you please to stay as close as possible to your cabin at night. Homesickness has been pretty bad with your campers at night. Two have been to the infirmary crying and said you weren't there. I will certainly appreciate your cooperation in this matter."

Tony: "Yes, Ma'am!"

Camp Director: "Thanks!"

(He leaves.)

The game was broken up because the director refused to have her attention turned away from Tony and his responsibility.

9
The Camp Director

The effectiveness of any camp is strongly influenced by the personality and planning of the camp director. My analysis of directors and my fifteen years of serving as a camp director convinces me these are important qualities of the person who is successful in filling this position:

1. Do concentrated study and planning months before camp takes place. In my early years of directing camp, it was propelled more by my energy, enthusiasm, and humor than by disciplined planning. Experience taught me that the broader base I laid in study and contact with people through organizations like Christian Camping International, the more depth and inspiration were felt by staff and campers the entire summer.

2. Enjoy camp as a participant, not merely as a director who tells others what to do. It was my goal never to direct camp from the office. I played ball, jumped hurdles, went hiking, and participated in cookouts and in every phase of camp life I could. Involvement in the camp activities will help a director to be sympathetic with staffers and make adjustments in work loads if needed. A director who is aware of what is going on can better handle conflicts and head off worse problems. His contact with campers will strengthen his insights about program planning and his concern for campers.

3. Discipline and confront as the need arises. Doing the thing that is best for the overall spirit of camp without undue concern over being popular with either staffers or campers is essential. When a counselor has difficulty controlling his cabin, sometimes the director needs to give guidance to the counselor. Sometimes the director needs to step in and talk directly with the campers or initiate some discipline, such as having them do extra cleanup duty or pick up pinecones until they work off excess energy. When

staffers are careless about duties, the director needs to counsel with those involved.

4. Be a growing person. The director who is opening his life to God daily so he can grow spiritually is much more apt to inspire others at camp to grow than the director who feels he has arrived. The director who confronts himself with his immaturities and seeks to grow emotionally will influence others towards emotional growth. If a director is excited about learning and developing new interests, he will likely have the capacity to generate in others new purpose and challenge. He will be a motivator.

5. Trust others and open avenues in programming that allow staffers and campers to express their talents. When I first began as director, I felt I must have *all* the ideas. Our programs back then remind me of somebody playing a one-string guitar. That one string was plucked all summer. I came to realize that the staff members were like an orchestra. Each one was an instrument filled with music. My job was to be the conductor and draw all the possible music out of each staffer and harmonize it. How rich our programs became!

Once a waterfront director called me over the speaker to say it looked cloudy. She asked if I thought that she should get the campers out of the lake. I told her, "I hired you to make that decision."

Too many Christian adults trust only themselves. As leaders, whether pastors or camp directors, they act as if they always know best. People working with such leaders do not grow. This approach can also lead to overwork by the director. It can cause tension and tiredness that result in a sour director whom people hate to approach.

An insecure leader cannot release responsibility and is threatened by the competence of others working with him. The view I received through being a counselor influenced me to guide my staff to do more teaching. I resented being a baby-sitter. I wanted more opportunities to teach and influence the campers spiritually. My staffers were given teaching duties.

6. Proceed with fairness and honesty. As a cabin counselor during my college years, I was struck by the favoritism I saw the camp director show to the lifeguards. At night, while the counselors kept the children and saw to their needs, the director often took the lifeguards out to get hamburgers and milkshakes. A sense of the need for balance in duties and fairness in privileges for all staffers emerged in my thinking.

A director needs to be a person of his word. What he promises to do, he should do. When he is at fault, he must admit this if people are to trust him. Willingness to consider the views of staffers and to respect differences seems essential to me.

7. The director needs a sense of humor. Being able to forget yourself and act silly is a renewing experience for most people. I can remember a particular staffer who sometimes said to me at Monday morning staff meetings, "Miss Sanders, make us laugh. I need it." As a leader of young people, I collected jokes and a few funny readings and often concentrated on seeing the funny side of things.

10
What to Look for
in Selecting Staffers

The process of selecting proper staff members for a Christian camp needs to begin months before the camping season. I sent publicity to religious directors on college campuses throughout the state. This was followed by planned visits to these campuses to interview prospects.

After applications were received, I began contacts with four to six references. It is true that securing adequate information about prospective staffers can be a problem. On many campuses a professor who is listed for a reference can probably tell something about regularity of class attendance and quality of work turned into him but may know nothing about the student personally. The religious director can tell whether the student attends regular religious activities, but in many instances cannot say much about the quality of his interactions with others and the characteristics of his personality.

If the student has a job, his supervisor or boss should be able to tell a camp director how dependable, thorough, and cooperative he is. Is he usually on time? Is he often absent? Does he perform his assigned tasks well?

Some contact with the pastor of the home church should provide information about the morals of the student and place of church in his life and the life of his family. Many pastors will know how cooperative the prospect is in his interactions with church members and church activities.

A personal interview with prospects is usually worth a considerable amount of time, money, and effort on the part of the camp director. Seeing the person tells something about his personal sense of pride and whether he appears to have a personality that will contact youth in a meaningful way in the setting of a Christian camp.

The director needs to have in mind some thought-provoking questions to ask prospects such as:

1. What would you expect to gain from a summer at a Christian camp?

2. What qualifications do you possess to be effective with youth at a Christian camp?

3. Tell me how Christ became real to you.

4. At this point in your life, what would you say is your main goal?

5. Tell me about a person who has influenced you and how.

6. Tell me about some of your interests or hobbies.

7. What do you consider to be some problem or difficulty you have faced? How did you cope?

8. Describe a time when you felt a sense of achievement. Why did you feel this way?

9. Can you share a funny or embarrassing experience that happened to you?

10. Do you have any fears you are willing to discuss?

In seeking staff members for a Christian camp, I think the director needs to look for these characteristics:

1. Emotional stability. I have had young people working with me who could be counted on to carry out their duties without asking themselves if they felt like doing that duty at a given time. They could cope well with the dailiness of life. They felt a sense of pride and fulfillment as they helped children with crafts or guarded them carefully as they laughed and swam in the lake. They studied and planned so that Bible study was made interesting. Such actions express the kind of emotional stability that are the key to effective camping.

There have been staffers working with me who expressed emotional stability by pulling with other staffers rather than competing against them. Such persons have enjoyed recognition when it came their way but have not felt they needed constantly to be "made over."

When children begin to get homesick as the sun sinks down, they cry and can become quite demanding. At that time an emotionally mature counselor can listen, understand, and act firmly. When a cut foot becomes cause for mass hysteria, the stable counselor calmly gives reassurance.

Energy and enthusiasm characterize the healthy person. Such a person likes himself and likes others. He knows that he is not perfect and that others are not perfect. He recognizes his strengths and develops these. He can compliment others on what they do well. He accepts his imperfections and allows them to help him develop humility. Being in touch with his weakness generates compassion for the failures and irritations of others.

The person of emotional stability can accept some criticism. He learns from his mistakes. He does not escape into physical illness or drugs when things do not go his way.

A director needs to know if the prospective staffer is going in some predictable direction. Do his goals and behavior fit together? Does he appear to have some stable values that give direction to his life? Is his behavior erratic, or is he basically consistent in his loyalties?

Nothing about a staff member can make up for a lack of basic emotional stability.

2. A personal encounter with Christ that can be shared and that is lived out in wholesome moral values and loving relationships. Certainly references should indicate participation in church and/or religious activities on campus.

Prospective staffers who run around with the crowd that is known to drink, to take drugs, and to live sexually loose lives should be highly suspect. Having high morals but being cold and aloof in personality will not communicate Christ in the best way at camp.

Communicating Christ to young people at camp involves spiritual understanding that is rooted in a practical faith. Staffers who value Bible truths and pray regularly must relate these activities to daily life if they are to influence campers in a healthy way.

3. A personality that is winsome and attractive. Winsomeness includes interest in people that is expressed in reaching out to others. Staffers will need to be able to converse and feel at home in a new setting. If staffers are withdrawn or overly self-conscious, they will have difficulty expressing interest in the hobbies, families, and problems of campers.

Attractiveness can be measured by appearance, manner, and enthusiasm for life. The more talents and interests wrapped up in a staff, the greater the potential for a fruitful summer. I can remember staffers who played varied musical instruments, who could rewrite skits to suit our need, who could entertain with songs they wrote, and who could mimic or role-play, to the delight of campers.

Winsome and attractive people who represent Christ are much more apt to draw people to him than boring, unkempt, and colorless persons.

4. Some leadership potential. In listing this requirement, I am talking about the ability to make decisions without having to ask. Orientation, a staff guidebook, and some help with individual matters on occasion should be sufficient.

A staff member may be so insecure that he winds up expecting others to make all his decisions for him. This can become a hardship. Each staffer has enough matters to decide in his particular job. We will expect staffers to grow in judgment and leadership throughout the summer.

The people who are found to work at a Christian camp will not be perfect. It will be a challenge each day to seek to love, mold, and believe in staffers. They are, however, a camp director's most valuable asset, or his most binding liability.

11
Preventing Burnout Among Staffers

Burnout has become a familiar term. It usually refers to a feeling of tired indifference. A person has given until he feels empty. He feels he has nothing else to give. Such a person has not taken care to get his own needs met while seeking to help others.

A hot summer of giving out guidance, love, and support can produce burnout rather quickly. It takes much energy to inspire young people enough to ensure participation in a camp program. Answering a million questions a day, settling disputes, and coping with homesickness and griping can tax the most patient staff members.

Based on my experiences as a camp director and my knowledge of mental health, I make these suggestions to prevent burnout among staff:

1. Plan special morale builders as the need indicates. I remember a week at camp when my camp staff members were fed up with campers who spent every meal complaining about food that was adequate and tasty. We normally had campers choose a table the second meal and eat there the entire week. This cut down on confusion. It took less time to get settled for eating. People who ate all meals together had a chance to get better acquainted as the week passed.

When the staff insisted they had had it with the complaining at meals, we had "fruit basket turnover" and changed eating places. This helped. We also started a gratitude emphasis. We fixed some hats with a label "I am a griper." These were to be worn by campers who complained at meals. Both campers and staffers were soon in better spirits. Sometimes the staff needs a party with homemade ice cream and cakes, while the director or other staff take turns checking cabins. We used to do this at times after lights-out at night.

Sometimes when activities were lagging, I would announce at mealtime that I was challenging the camp pastor and some missionaries to a game of shuffleboard. The young people would gather to watch. We made announcements about winners in the dining hall.

There are times when the director needs to talk to the staff about certain problems that are hurting morale or to present mentally and spiritually challenging devotional thoughts. Some fresh and different experience of praying together as a staff can be renewing. (See chap. 2 of this book for suggestions.)

2. Have good food. We used to have dietitians who planned meals with canned vegetables. Later, a dietitian from a community near camp made contacts with farmers in the area to furnish fresh fruits and vegetables. The cooks began making homemade rolls once a day, and these were always a big hit.

When we had a certain meat the staff members called "mystery meat," they used to tease about hoping they would not be called on to thank God for the food.

Of course, we had some campers who complained regardless of what we had to eat. However, the overall spirit of camp was better if the food was good and if there was enough of it. Staff members who were at camp all summer were especially influenced by good or poor food.

3. Make meetings organized and to the point. No meeting should be called unless it has a purpose. What is to be covered at a meeting needs some organization before it is held. As soon as the purpose of the meeting is achieved, it should be concluded. Sometimes leaders seem to have an ego problem. They like to hear themselves talk whether they have anything to say or not.

Many worship times are ruined by too much talking about matters that need to be covered at other times. We used to make most announcements at lunchtime. I can remember a missionary commenting on how refreshing it was to him that I could get to the point and sit down. He had just been in a camp that had an excellent program, but he said the announcements took an unbelievable amount of time. He had found this annoying. Some leaders need notes to glance at so they cover everything smoothly.

4. Compliment staffers and help them with their problems. I believe a camp director needs to take a personal interest in every staffer. If a staffer is depressed, the director needs to show the kind of concern that opens the door for the sharing of a problem. Surely camp directors need to be growing every year in knowledge of human relations and counseling skills. Obviously, not all staffers will wish to confide in the director. This decision should be left completely with the staffer.

When staffers contribute to the program, they should be noticed and commended. When they handle camper problems with poise and maturity, they should be affirmed. If staff members teach Bible study, I believe the director should visit around enough that he knows what kind of teaching is going on and can comment on it.

If staffers need suggestions, these can be collected and shared in a general way or shared with individuals. Many camp directors will be experienced teachers but need to be tolerant of the inexperience of staffers. Also, people teach differently. Room for individuality will be needed. Teaching helps should be covered well before camp and a bibliography of resources provided each teacher.

5. Plan time off so staffers can be completely away from the camp at adequate intervals. Camp life is confining. It involves responsibility for campers twenty-four hours a day. The world of camp means adjusting to many different personalities. Without adequate time away, staff members can easily become irritable and also lose their sense of purpose.

A Christian camp setting can be pretty unrealistic compared to the world outside. Times of being back as a part of the outside world are important.

When I was first a camp staff member, our camp ran from Monday to Monday. The only time off we had was one afternoon or evening a week. I can remember times when we felt we would scream if a camper made one more demand. For staff members who have little free time, there then is often added the load of guilt for being unloving.

I remember a time when a fellow staff member and I had one activity period free every day. We tried to go where we would be free of campers' demands—a healthy thing to do! Every little adventure away from responsibility was refreshing.

During the fifteen years that I was camp director, we had part of Saturday and Sunday off. Most of the staff left camp for weekends. It was good for them to reestablish contact with family and friends away from camp. Going shopping at a mall was a contrast to the retreat existence at camp. I was made aware, when I left camp for the weekend, that I had been absorbed to a point unconscious to me. Prolonged confinement at camp is not healthy.

6. Build variety into the camp program. I used to think that planning a program and sticking to it cut down on the output of energy. I discovered that more energy is lost through monotony and boredom than through variety that requires extra thought and effort.

The monotony of a program affects people much like rocking down a highway in a cruise-controlled car on a sunny day. You begin to get so sleepy that you almost run off the road. You develop the feeling that the car could run itself with no help from you. A very routine program runs off the road of effectiveness. Staffers become so bored that they begin to feel the program has surely developed enough know-how to propel itself. They begin dragging to the craft hut to take charge. They begin sitting by while telling the campers how to shoot archery or play tennis. They begin writing letters on the waterfront instead of watching campers who are swimming. They decide to stay in their cabin during the showing of the movies they have memorized. There is the tired feeling, "I just can't stand to hear and see that same movie again."

In the meantime, such lethargy on the part of the staff affects campers with a desire to lie on the bunks instead of shooting archery. Campers who start a ball game wind up miserable because they are fighting over the rules. Without supervision, they may become frustrated and go back to their cabins. When campers show up excited about making a craft item and the staffer is fifteen minutes late, or does not offer the help needed to learn the craft, enthusiasm can degenerate into complaining.

The results of such staffer neglect can lead to camper homesickness. Uninvolvement is one of the key contributions to homesickness.

A balance needs to be struck between all new activities while also relying on some established activities that require less thought. Rotating activities from week to week helps. Using four or five different themes and theme songs during a summer can generate sufficient balance.

7. Work out some arrangement that will allow time for staffers to fellowship with each other. We looked forward to being together for staff meetings. The campers cleaned up cabins after breakfast, and this was when we had our meeting. The more privacy you can have for such meetings, the better. We were close enough to be contacted if needed by any of the campers, but our time together as a staff was special; and our oneness of spirit and purpose was strengthened as a result.

Our counselors helped every morning for one period with crafts, recreation, or nature study. The second period in the morning and the afternoon were free for them. The lifeguards were on the waterfront both periods morning and afternoon, but they were free of the campers when they went to their living quarters.

We had two cabins per building with a counselor's room between them. Two counselors roomed together. The lifeguards lived in what we called the staff house. They were not responsible for devotional times at night, although they seemed to like being invited to conduct these at times. They did not have to keep a cabin quiet at rest hour or at night. Instead, they could be together in the staff house and visit during both these times. The musicians, the recreation director, and the nature director had pretty much the same free times as the lifeguards. They, too, lived in the staff house.

8. Allow for fun but not for so many practical jokes that they get completely out of hand.

When I first became a camp director, I thought practical jokes were "all the go." There was a rash of throwing people into the lake, a dangerous thing to do! I had a red slip that constantly disappeared from my drawer and reappeared on the flagpole. The staff locked all my clothes in the trading post while I was taking a shower before the evening meal. People found pinecones in their beds. Watermelon fights were common.

Practical jokes can be dangerous and irritating. Have you ever had a busy day of chasing campers all over a hillside, fallen into bed exhausted, and failed to see the humor of lying down on a gritty bed or one full of pinecones? I have seen tempers flare because practical jokes were carried too far.

9. Emphasize the value of regular exercise. Staff members need to develop the daily discipline of exercise. This makes people more alert mentally. It is also an avenue for letting off emotional steam. About thirty minutes daily of some aerobic exercise—jogging, swimming, bicycling, or brisk walking—has been proven to enhance a positive self-image. Such exercise can spur creative thought and increase energy level. It is helpful in preventing heart trouble.

10. Even though you work at a religious camp, do not spiritualize overmuch. Reading the Bible and quoting Scripture are fine things to do, but a constant diet of both is unhealthy.

Staff members who do cross-stitch or read novels in their free time are likely to do more to renew themselves than if they are always reading the Bible. Camp is a great place to get interested in the study of birds and butterflies. Many of my staff members brought their hobbies with them to camp and also developed new ones.

12
Choral Readings

Choral readings can be used as a part of any worship experience. They can carry out the theme of one particular emphasis or of the entire camp program for a week.

The effective way to prepare for a choral reading is to choose people with good speaking voices and teach them to speak out clearly, distinctly, and loudly. If more than one person is to say any phrase, sentence, or group of sentences together, they will need to practice and learn unity. When phrases are picked up by incoming voices, there should be only brief pauses between if people are to catch the continuity of what is said.

A leader needs to plan the choral readings, give copies to all who are to participate, and set up enough rehearsals that there is smoothness in the presentation. Memorizing a choral reading will make it easier to command the attention of an audience. However, adequate familiarity with a choral reading that is read can allow participants to look up often. This is important if it is to be presented with meaning and communicated to the audience.

Conducting a discussion of the message of a choral reading with those who are to present it might help them to speak out with more expression.

Choral Reading 1: Jesus Shall Reign

All: Jesus shall reign!
First Voice: Where?
All: Over all the world!
Second Voice: What right has he to reign?
All: He is Creator and Lord of the universe!
Third Voice: He made the trees.
Second Voice: The birds and butterflies;
First Voice: The cats and bees;
Second Voice: The mountains and the skies.
All: He made the sun and moon.

Third Voice: He made the stars also.
All: Yes, he is Creator!
First Voice: He breathed into man the very breath of life.
All: And man was created in the image of God.
Second Voice: Possessor of a soul, a free will, and a creative mind.
First and Second Voices: Does Jesus reign in your heart and life?
Third Voice: You mean, is he the ruler and commander of my life?
First and Second Voices: Yes!
Third Voice: I love God better than anyone.
Second Voice: How do you show such love?
Third Voice: I talk to him each day and tell others of his love. I serve him through his church—give my money, talents, and service through his church!
First Voice: Do you feed the hungry, clothe the poor, and visit the lonely about you?
Third Voice: Yes!
All: "Inasmuch as ye have done it unto one of the least of these, my brethren, ye have done it unto me" (Matt. 25:40), said Jesus.
First and Second Voices: Do you insist on having *your own way,* or is *his will* more important?
Third Voice: His will comes first, for he is Lord!
All: There are many pompous, wealthy rulers in the world today.
First Voice: Yes, and gods of stone and wood.
Second Voice: Many worship the Allah of Islam and bow before him five times daily.
Third Voice: Many know not the true God, God in the human life of Jesus Christ of Nazareth.
All: "There is no other name under heaven given among men by which we must be saved" (Acts 4:12, RSV).

First Voice: One day Jesus shall reign over all the world.

Second Voice: "For great is the Lord, and greatly to be praised;/he is to be feared above all gods."

All: "For all the gods of the peoples are idols; but the Lord made the heavens."

Third Voice: "Worship the Lord in holy array;/tremble before him, all the earth!"

All: "Say among the nations, 'The Lord reigns!'" (Ps. 96:4-5,9-10a, RSV).

Choral Reading 2: The Walls

First Voice: There are walls around gardens,
Second Voice: Walls around homes,
Third Voice: Walls around schools,
Fourth Voice: Walls around convents,
Fifth Voice: Walls to close people in,
Sixth Voice: Walls to shut people out, and
Seventh Voice: Walls for protection.
First Voice: There are walls that are many years old,
Second Voice: Walls just recently raised,
Third Voice: Walls around castles,
Fourth Voice: Walls around mansions,
Fifth Voice: Walls around cottages,
Sixth Voice: Walls around farms,
Seventh Voice: And walls in people's hearts!
First Voice: There's the wall of indifference—
Second Voice: Indifference that says, "You go your way and I'll go mine."
Third Voice: "So you are hungry, dirty, illiterate . . ."
Fourth Voice: "If you had more pride and weren't lazy,"
Fifth Voice: "You could lift yourself and get off welfare."
Sixth Voice: "People who want to amount to something do."
Seventh Voice: "People who care are clean."
First Voice: There are walls of prejudice that separate people.
Second Voice: That judge them by color, by clothes, by neighborhood.
Third Voice: Black makes you different.
Fourth Voice: White makes you my enemy.
Fifth Voice: Jewish means you're a cheat.
Sixth Voice: Being poorly dressed makes you trashy,
Seventh Voice: Inferior, and unimportant.
First Voice: There are walls inside hearts
Second Voice: Because of fear.
Third Voice: I want to know you,
Fourth Voice: But I don't know how.
Fifth Voice: How do I build a bridge

Sixth Voice: From my world to yours?
Seventh Voice: How can we learn to trust and truly communicate?
First Voice: There are walls of self-pity that close people tightly inside themselves.
Second Voice: That make their problems bigger than those of anybody else.
Third Voice: Walls that say, "Nobody is as bad off as I."
Fourth Voice: Walls that make me useless.
Fifth Voice: Selfish and helpless.
Sixth Voice: Walls that keep people from seeing
Seventh Voice: That there are sick people while they are well.
First Voice: There are poor people, while they have enough.
Second Voice: There are hungry people, while they are full.
Third Voice: There are blind people, while they can see;
Fourth Voice: Deaf people, while they can hear;
Fifth Voice: Mute people,while they can talk;
Sixth Voice: Paralyzed people, while they can walk.
Seventh Voice: Oh, the walls of self-pity would drop away
All: If people could see the many needs of others and their mission to service.
First Voice: There are walls of lovelessness in the hearts of many,
Second Voice: Who simply want power and position for themselves.
Third Voice: Who will run over the helpless and needy,
Fourth Voice: Who have no sensitivity for the feelings of others;
Fifth Voice: Who do not know how to value friends, family, and associates.
Sixth Voice: The good of the children means nothing to them,
Seventh Voice: Only that they should add to the prestige of the parents.
First Voice: The walls of guilt are high in the lives of many.
Second Voice: They are there because some young people have abused their bodies.
Third Voice: Torn down the nobility of their place in society.
Fourth Voice: Guilt has raised walls due to dishonesty, filthy talk,
Fifth Voice: Habits that destroy health and Christian influence.
Sixth Voice: Some face a wall of guilt because they've

put the crowd above God and the church.

Seventh Voice: They've been careless about duties and opportunities,

All: Knowing all the while God demands our very best!

Confession: (The person presiding will ask everyone to form a circle and hold hands. If they are willing to confess a weakness or sin to one next to them, they do. There is a period of silent prayer for these struggles made known to a neighbor. Remain in circle for rest of program.)

Solo: "Dear Lord and Father of Mankind" (270, *Baptist Hymnal*, 1975).

All: Praise to God who frees our souls, who tears down every wall. Whose love restores broken relationships, and tears down every wall. Who shows men how to be true brothers, and tears down every wall! The wall between us and God can be torn down through confession. Jesus' love and cleansing can free us, no matter what we've done.

First Voice: "And since we have a great priest over the house of God, let us draw near with a true heart in full assurance of faith with our hearts sprinkled clean from an evil conscience and our bodies washed with pure water. Let us hold fast the confession of our hope without wavering, for he who promised is faithful" (Heb. 10:21-23, RSV).

All: Praise to God, for through Christ every wall has been broken down!

Everybody sing: "Blest Be the Tie" (256, *Baptist Hymnal*, 1975).

I used this choral reading at a teenage encounter program. I had a photographer to make slides of all kinds of walls and fences. These were shown while the choral reading was being presented. We had a separate slide depicting each of the following, as they were talked about: (1) poor people in a rundown section of town, (2) blacks and whites, (3) a sick person, (4) a blind person with a cane, (5) a person in a wheelchair, (6) a person in a business office dressed in a suit, (7) a girl in revealing clothes being hugged by a long-haired boy in jeans.

Choral Reading 3: Seek First the Kingdom of God

First Character: I shall seek fame and applause as the primary goal of my life! I shall be lauded and envied for my popularity and power.

Backstage Voices: Seek first the kingdom of God!

First Character: My name will glitter in shining lights, and my picture will often be seen on magazine covers and in newspapers.

Backstage Voices: Seek first the kingdom of God!

First Character: Already I am the center of every party and acclaimed an actress of rare talent.

Backstage Voices: Seek first the kingdom of God!

Second Character: My goal in life is material wealth. If I have enough money, I can do anything!

Backstage Voices: Seek first the kingdom of God!

Second Character: I shall visit Paris, Rome, Venice, Tokyo—and many other great cities of the world. I shall enjoy great adventure and excitement all my life.

Backstage Voices: Seek first the kingdom of God!

Second Character: Money will buy me lovely clothes and beautiful cars. My position will be secure, and I shall have whatever I desire. Money will bring me happiness. I know it will!

Backstage Voices: Seek first the kingdom of God!

Third Character: Just a little home with several children and a handsome husband where I can find love is all I ask out of life.

Backstage Voices: Seek first the kingdom of God!

Third Character: I shall take good care of my children, feed them nutritious foods, rear them in a psychologically sound home, and give them the finest educational opportunities. My children will be well prepared to meet life.

Backstage Voices: Seek first the kingdom of God!

Fourth Character: I have died to self and desire only to do God's will! Since God is the Lord of the earth and of every individual life, I shall seek to live only that I might bring honor and praise to his name.

Backstage Voices: Of such is the kingdom of God!

Fourth Character: My life is not my own. I have been bought with the price of shed blood on a cruel cross, for my Savior loved me so.

Backstage Voices: He took upon himself our sin!

Fourth Character: Therefore, I dedicate my all to

Unison of Fourth Character and Backstage Voices: Seek first the kingdom of God!

Choral Reading 4: Shine for Me

Choral reading for a candlelighting service or campfire (This may be adapted for an installation.)

Music: solo, "Be Thou My Vision" (212, *Baptist Hymnal*, 1975)

All: Jesus said, "I am the light of the world" (John 8:12). Jesus said, "Ye are the light of the world" (Matt. 5:14).

First Voice: Light has always been a sign of goodness, purity, and truth.

Second Voice: Darkness has always been a sign of evil, sin, and lostness.

Third Voice: The deeds that are evil are often performed at night so they will not be seen.

Fourth Voice: The deeds of goodness need not be hidden. They may be done in the bright daylight, for they bring no shame!

First Voice: Jesus has been called the Light of the World because he is pure, true, righteous and good.

Second Voice: Jesus is like a light shining into every heart to help people see the evil in their hearts.

Third Voice: When they see their own sin and shame, they want to be washed by Jesus, who makes them pure and clean.

Fourth Voice: Then these who are cleansed become lights.

All: Jesus said, "Ye are the light of the world" (Matt. 5:14*a*). Go shine for me!

First Voice: How are we to let our lights shine?

Second Voice: By starting family worship in our homes.

Third Voice: By telling our lost friends about Jesus.

Fourth Voice: By reading our Bibles and praying for the missionaries each day,

All: By doing acts of kindness to the lonely and shut-ins,

First Voice: By being loyal to our churches,

All: By doing only what will honor Jesus Christ, our Savior and Lord!

(All sing "Send the Light" or "Pass It On" [304 or 287, *Baptist Hymnal*, 1975], as the candles are lighted.)

Choral Reading 5: The Missionary

All: How shall they hear without a preacher?

First and Fourth Voices: The missionary speaks and, wondering, we follow the path of his words

First Voice: Into the red man's tent of rebellion and disbelief . . .

Second Voice: The black man's grass hut of ignorance and superstition . . .

Third Voice: The adobe of the brown man's ritual and fear . . .

Fourth Voice: The Oriental shrine of idols and mysticism . . .

Fifth Voice: The islander's shack of lethargy and confusion . . .

All: Or any man's house of sin and woe!

First and Fourth Voices: His a divine appointment for a labor of love,

First and Second Voices: Rampant with heartaches and profuse with disappointments we can never understand,

Fifth and Sixth Voices: Alive with joys and pleasures we can never know.

First and Fourth Voices: His vision is strangely limited to the heart and its potential under grace.

Third and Fourth Voices: He moves over into the world of the alien and finds there his "Home, Sweet Home"—

Fifth and Sixth Voices: God's love, the key that opens every treasure.

All: "And how shall they preach, except they be sent?"

First and Fourth Voices: They who serve must look— not for the shining path of another's service, but, rather, to the glowing charge from God's own direction.

First and Second Voices: We dare not defile the word of God with human sympathies or planned ambitions;

Fifth and Sixth Voices: They can never provide safe passage into realms of his "unknown" . . .

Third and Fourth Voices: Nor the power to reach and to bind the sin-sores of the world.

Sixth Voice: His call may be for dedication to pray the way or pay the way that others may learn of Christ's love.

First and Second Voices: For every one who goes, there must be many to stay.

First and Fourth Voices: To all the glory of "laborers together with God."

All: "Blest be the tie"—the glistening cord that binds our hearts and our hands around the world!

—Mary N. Taylor
(Printed in *The Commission*; reprinted by permission from *The Commission*; arranged as a choral reading by Marjorie Sanders.)

13
Dramas

Drama 1: Conflict

This is a three-act drama concerning:

(1) MOTHER-DAUGHTER CONFLICT

(2) SUNDAY SCHOOL TEACHER-TEEN CONFLICT (concerning biblical standards about sex and popular standards)

(3) EMPLOYER-EMPLOYEE CONFLICT

The most effective way to present this drama will be for a skilled leader to conduct a discussion with the audience between each act. Such a leader needs to exercise calmness and be competent in using the clarifying response.

A leader will need to lay down some guidelines with the audience before the drama begins. These guidelines might include:

(1) No person will interrupt while another is speaking.

(2) Keep the tone of voice loud enough so all present can hear but not raised with the kind of emotionalism that tries to dominate with one person's view.

(3) Treat all views with respect, recognizing that every person present has the right to his own view. No making fun or cutting down of any person's view should be tolerated.

(4) Stress the fact that views should be expressed freely, but that a spirit of goodwill must be the primary goal.

If this play is presented at a teen camp, you might want to make it a part of a parent visitation program so both teenagers and parents can engage in the discussions. Such a program could also be effective as a local church activity.

You might wish to allow campers to discuss each act by small groups. Each cabin could gather in a group led by several staffers and discuss in individual groups. Such an arrangement would likely create more participation, better conditions for hearing, and a more attentive response on the part of all present. This type of arrangement could be used with parent/teen programs where you prepare small group leaders ahead of time. Also, such a discussion might be freer if the parents of a particular teenager are not in the same group with him.

Episode 1: Mother-Daughter Conflict

Characters: Betty, a teenage girl about thirteen to fifteen years of age, wearing jeans.

Mother, about thirty-five years old, dressed for doing housework.

Setting: An arrangement that looks like a typical living room with a TV.

(As the curtain opens, Betty is watching TV. Her mother enters and addresses her.)

Mother: Young lady, is that all you have to do, watch TV? Have you looked at your room lately?

Betty: No, Mother, I haven't looked at it. I've been sleeping in the garage. Tell me about it!

Mother: All right. Don't get smart with me! You are old enough to contribute to the orderliness around here, but your room looks like a pigpen! Your clothes are piled everywhere. Your bed isn't made; and when did you last change your linen?

Betty: Mother, did it ever occur to you *that is my room*? I should be able to leave it the way I choose.

Mother: But *your room* is a part of this house! And if anybody sees it, they will think you've never been taught anything.

Betty: All you ever think about is what people think! Who cares what they think?

Mother: One day you will care, young lady. Your reputation in a community means everything. It determines what social activities you're included in and even influences people concerning your future job. I'm thinking of *your* welfare.

Betty: Mother, you are *so hung up* on fitting into the mold that you don't even know who you are inside. I don't want to be pushed into somebody else's idea of who I should be. I have unique gifts, and I need to discover and develop these in a way that will allow my creativity to evolve. Look at you! You aren't really happy. You attend a bridge club every week and come home griping about how boring it is. But you must keep in line with your neighbors with money, position, and prestige.

Mother: Well, yes, I do gripe sometimes about the bridge club; but the contact with these friends is important.

Betty: I question your use of the term friends. To me friends are people we know from deep inside. We know and accept the weaknesses and struggles of each other. We aren't competing with each other for prestige. We can do simple things together, like hiking in the woods, making a snowman, and laughing and sharing freely.

Mother: Oh, sure, friends! Friends like Tim, your hippie friend who looks like he is destitute when he can afford to wear good-looking clothes. It's beyond me how you could be attracted to such a tramp! In my day we were impressed with neat, sharp-looking men who knew how to dress.

Betty: That's exactly why your lives are so superficial. Tim has an attractiveness that is deeper. I have made contact with a person, not a wardrobe!

Mother: It's obvious we won't ever resolve this conflict!

(Curtain closes.)

(While the scene is being changed, you could have a group to play and sing "Go Gently Through the Years," by Diane L. Rutledge, page 42, *Sing 'N' Celebrate.*)

Discussion Time

Episode 2: Sunday School Teacher-Teen Conflict
    Characters: Mrs. Ayers, the Sunday School teacher
                         Debbie
                         Susan
                         Gina   fourteen- and fifteen-year-old
                                          teenage girls
                         Joanne
                         Linda
Setting: A typical Sunday School classroom with a small table and six chairs.

(As the episode opens, it is obvious that a discussion is going on.)

Mrs. Ayers: You mean, you girls see nothing wrong with going to bed with a boy before you marry him?

Debbie: That's right, as long as the two love each other.

Mrs. Ayers: How would you girls define love?

Debbie: Love is wanting to be with somebody.

Susan: To me, it means there's kind of a magic quality about doing simple things together.

Joanne: If you love somebody, you miss that person when you are separated. You can hardly wait to see him again.

Gina: And loving somebody involves expressing it. My boyfriend told me if I loved him, I would want to be affectionate with him. There's something wrong with somebody who doesn't want to express his love.

Mrs. Ayers: I've heard from everybody but Linda. Linda, how would you define love?

Linda: I don't know.

Mrs. Ayers: I see. Well, I agree love involves wanting to be with the person you love, enjoying his company, and expressing that love. However, even though expressing love physically is normal and right, to me there are some laws of God that govern when and with whom this should take place. Let's get our Bibles and read a few passages. Turn to 1 Corinthians 6:9-10. Linda, please read this out loud. I believe you have the Revised Version, don't you?

Linda: Yes.

Mrs. Ayers: OK, Linda. Read verses 9 and 10.

Linda: "Do you not know that the unrighteous will not inherit the kingdom of God? Do not be deceived; neither the immoral, nor idolaters, nor adulterers, nor sexual perverts, nor thieves, nor the greedy, nor drunkards, nor revilers, nor robbers will inherit the kingdom of God."

Mrs. Ayers: Thank you. Now, Joanne, please read from your Revised Standard Version 1 Corinthians 6:18-20.

Joanne: "Shun immorality. Every other sin which a man commits is outside the body; but the immoral man sins against his own body. Do you not know that your body is a temple of the Holy Spirit within you, which you have from God? You are not your own; you were bought with a price. So glorify God in your body."

Debbie: What does adultery really mean?

Mrs. Ayers: Adultery refers to people who are married having intercourse with people other than their marriage partner.

Debbie: Actually, that passage does not include people who aren't married, then. It mentions adulterers and homosexuals.

Mrs. Ayers: The passage in 1 Corinthians 6:9-10 also lists the immoral.

Susan: What does that mean?

Mrs. Ayers: I looked it up last night in the dictionary; and it said immorality was a state of wickedness, vice, or unchastity. Chastity deals with being a virgin, or one who has not had intercourse. So, to me, the passage means that those who will not inherit the kingdom of God could include, not only adulterers and homosexuals, but those who have intercourse and are not married.

Joanne: I agree, too, that it is important to keep our bodies pure. My father says he could not have trusted my mother if he knew she wasn't a virgin when they married.

Gina: I think that is as old-timey as it can be! If you love somebody and plan to marry him, what difference does it make whether you go through a ceremony or sign a piece of paper before you go to bed together?

Debbie: Sure! There are lots of people who live together before they get married, and that way they find out for sure if they are sexually compatible.

Mrs. Ayers: A woman involved in such a situation faces several problems. In the first place, some of the factual books I've read about sex say that most women are not able to relax and have a satisfactory experience with sex outside the security of a marriage relationship. Such women can have frightening experiences with sex outside of wedlock that actually make them feel abnormal. Women are so designed that they find love and commitment a far more important part of sex than men. Men will say the required words of love, to secure the intimate relationship; but the entire situation is apt to be far more serious for the woman than for the man. Also, have you thought of the risk that you might become pregnant? What if the boy will not marry you, or you aren't ready to marry him?

Gina: We can always take birth control pills.

Mrs. Ayers: In the book *Sin, Sex, and Self-Control,* Dr. Norman Vincent Peale says there is lots of proof that girls who feel they are in love are often controlled unconsciously by a desire to have their lover's baby. A girl will carelessly leave off safeguards and, in many cases, become pregnant. Surveys, while in many ways inadequate, say that in many cases, the person who has intercourse for the first time has not planned it and has taken no precautions. I feel that every baby deserves a secure home where parents love and trust each other. A child conceived out of wedlock runs a greater risk of not having this stable home. To me, the most important word related to love is *responsibility.* When you are young, it is natural to stress only the warm, happy feelings that go with love; but there are responsibilities in building a home that depend on

commitment, trust, and self-discipline. The fact that my husband and I loved each other and could wait until we were married to become one physically demonstrated a mature sense of discipline and responsibility.

Joanne: It will take lots of responsibility to be good mothers. I want my children to be able to trust me and look up to me like I look up to my mother.

Susan: Your children won't expect the same standards of you that you did of your mother. This is a different age. I think it's just hard for adults to realize times have changed.

Mrs. Ayers: Paul wrote the two books of Corinthians. He was writing to people who lived among a pagan society that believed in free sex. We live today amid a society that is insisting we should loosen our standards. I say it's the same situation Paul faced. I say God's moral laws are as unchanging as his law of gravity. We don't break God's laws. They break us when we ignore them.

(Curtain closes.)
Discussion Time

Episode 3: Employer-Employee Conflict
   Characters: Mr. Brown, manager of the grocery store where Johnny works
            Johnny, a teenage boy
Setting: Grocery store
(Johnny is talking on the phone as the curtain opens.)

Johnny: Jill, you are something else! (Laughs.)
(Mr. Brown arrives on the scene.)

Mr. Brown: Johnny, could you please hang up? They need you at the front!

Johnny (Putting hand over phone and whispering to Mr. Brown): Just a minute.

Mr. Brown: I said, they need you right now!

Johnny: OK, OK! Jill, I've got to go. Bye!

Mr. Brown: Johnny, I'm afraid I'm going to be forced to fire you unless you improve.

Johnny: Ah, Mr. Brown, don't be unreasonable! Please don't fire me! I need the job!

Mr. Brown: You don't act like you need the job!

Johnny: My gosh! I have been working like a Trojan. Can I help it if I had a phone call?

Mr. Brown: You and I have discussed this enough times that, by now, you should have already told your friends to talk to you other times than when you are at work. Do you know how many times you've answered the phone already this afternoon?

Johnny: Oh, a couple of times, I guess.

Mr. Brown: No, four times; and when I just now

stopped you, that was a total of one solid hour you have talked on the phone instead of working.

Johnny: I know I haven't talked that much!

Mr. Brown: I made it a point to keep a record and to time you. The reason was that three times this week cashiers have complained to me you weren't available to bag groceries when they needed you.

Johnny: All adults are alike. They don't want teens to have any fun! You are nothing but a slave driver. I quit! (He throws down his apron and storms out. The curtain closes.)

Discussion Time

Drama 2: Hold Out Your Light

A CANDLELIGHT PLAY

Setting: The play should be presented after dark to be effective. Every person attending should be given a candle as he enters. (It will be wise to use cardboard holders attached to each candle to prevent burned hands and marred floors.) I suggest that you have a long table covered with a white or solid-colored sheet. This should be in the middle of the platform toward the front. Place large pieces of fern or branches of pine all along the edge of the platform, on top of the piano, and on the table.

Line up an arrangement of candles in holders on the table. Put a fourteen-inch white candle in the middle, one blue twelve-inch candle on each side, one red or orange twelve-inch candle on each side beside the blues, and one green ten-inch candle on either side of these on each end. This makes a total of seven candles needed, and be sure to have matches handy.

Use a lighted world globe in front of the table on the floor. Have the meeting place dark, except for the globe, center white candle, and one or two lighted candles near the piano. Have the choir seated to the side of the platform near the piano. A music director should direct the music and have the choir and pianist ready to come in on time.

Have enough copies of *Sing 'N' Celebrate* for all musicians. (All the music for this play is listed in *Sing 'N' Celebrate.*) See that the choir and pianist have adequate flashlights by which to see and that someone turns pages for the pianist.

Characters: Have six young people to be the speakers. Have an adult leader and reader. It is suggested that girls wear dresses and boys semi-dress up for the presentation.

As those attending are directed in, each person is given a candle and ushered down so every seat is filled. The pianist plays "Be Thou My Vision," page 33, and then switches to "Hold Out Your Light," page 86. When everyone has been seated, the choir sings "Hold Out Your Light."

(Leader comes to center of stage behind the table and stands there until the close of the service.)

Leader (Picks up middle candle): This candle is a symbol of the life of Christ. Jesus said, "I have come as light into the world, that whoever believes in me may not remain in darkness" (John 12:46, RSV). Young people are valuable in spreading the light of the gospel to a world in darkness. There is a service to be rendered in youth that cannot be given in adulthood.

Marie Bultmiere, a poor German immigrant, went into homes to sew and clean when she was fifteen. She used this as an opportunity to talk with people among whom she worked about her faith in Christ. She lived out that faith in daily contacts.

The prophet Jeremiah was called by God to be his spokesman. Jeremiah made excuses: "Then I said, 'Ah, Lord God! Behold, I do not know how to speak, for I am only a youth.' But the Lord said to me,/'Do not say, "I am only a youth"; for to all to whom I send you you shall go,/and whatever I command you you shall speak./Be not afraid of them, for I am with you to deliver you,/says the Lord'" (Jer. 1:6-8, RSV).

So God calls youth today to serve him; but he promises to go ahead of them to show the way. He promises to empower and glorify himself through those who are obedient to share the light of truth and love.

Choir sings: "Keep Me True," page 30.

(Enter Speaker 1.)

Speaker 1: If young people expect their lives to reflect Christ, they must have seen themselves in the light of God's purity and holiness. Such a vision leads to a cry of repentance and humility. But it also leads to a deep understanding of God's loving acceptance. Before we ever reach up to God, he is reaching down to us. God reached into the life of Florence Nightingale when she was still a young woman.

Growing up in a wealthy home, Florence had opportunities for travel and an exciting social life. But the time Florence loved best was when her family gave a large Christmas party for needy children. It was through ministering to others that she found meaning in her life. As a child, she dreamed of being a nurse, so she doctored broken dolls and crippled animals.

One day in a chapel on the Nightingale estate, Florence felt God calling her into his service. She surrendered, but her parents were alarmed. They wanted her to marry one of her wealthy boyfriends. She refused. They sent her abroad, hoping a trip would get her mind off being a nurse; but it did not.

When the call came for nurses to go to the battlefield to help the dying British soldiers fighting the Russians in the Crimean War, Florence volunteered. There she found wounded and dying soldiers piled in a foul, old, abandoned building. Enlisting help, she cleaned the place and demanded medicine. Late at night her lantern could be seen bobbing up and down the rows of suffering men. They called her an angel of mercy.

She was an ordinary woman, Florence Nightingale; but when the light of God's grace entered her life, he transformed her. She became his lightbearer. (Picks up candle beside the center one and lights it from center candle.) I light this candle in honor of the grace that enters hearts through surrender to do God's work in the world.

(Exit speaker 1.)

Choir sings: "Reach Out and Touch," page 29.

(Reader enters and stands beside Leader. She remains here throughout service, except they both step back out of the way as others speak.)

Reader: "In the beginning was the Word, and the Word was with God, and the Word was God. He was in the beginning with God; all things were made through him, and without him was not anything made that was made. In him was life, and the life was the light of men. The light shines in the darkness, and the darkness has not overcome it" (John 1:1-5, RSV).

(Enter speaker 2, from opposite side than speaker 1. Each speaker should alternate sides.)

Speaker 2: If young people intend to be God's lights, they must remember that their talents are not their own. God is the owner of all gifts. When these are entrusted to us, we must invest them as God directs. If we do not, we never realize the maximum development and blessedness of such gifts.

From an early age, Marian Anderson sang in the choir of a Baptist church in Philadelphia, Pennsylvania. Marian's father died when she was young, and her mother found it hard to provide for the needs of her family. It seemed that people quickly realized that Marian's voice was extraordinary.

She won scholarships and was sent on a concert tour to Europe, where there were standing ovations. Marian Anderson returned to America a celebrated singer. But the fact that Marian was black created problems in her native land. Efforts by Marian's manager to arrange a concert in Constitution Hall in Washington met with opposition. An outdoor concert was staged at the Lincoln Memorial.

The crowd of 75,000 stood to hear Marian sing "My Country, 'Tis of Thee," "Nobody Knows the Trouble I've Seen" as tears streamed down many faces. Her talent, given back to God, has brought honor to his name. (Lights candle beside large, middle candle, a blue one, from the lighted middle candle.) I light this candle to remind us of those whose talents are dedicated to God.

(Exit speaker 2.)

Choir sings: "The Greatest Gift," page 61.

(Enter speaker 3.)

Speaker 3: Ida Scudder grew up in the country of India, where her parents were missionaries. Ida came to America to study. She enjoyed the luxury and social life afforded her here. In fact, she had already decided never to return to India. However, a wire came saying her father needed her immediately because her mother was desperately ill; Ida must return to India to keep house for the family. She reluctantly dropped her studies and returned home. While she was there, God spoke to her through one night's strange events.

There was a knock on the door. A man standing on her doorstep begged Ida to come quickly and minister to his very ill wife. Ida tried to explain that it was her father who was the doctor. She would send him as soon as he returned home. The man insisted. His beliefs would not allow a man doctor to treat his wife. She said she was not trained to doctor people. He went away downcast.

The same experience occurred again two more times with two other men. In all, three men came that night to beg Ida for help. The next morning she heard the noises of funeral processions and recognized the same three men walking beside the caskets of their dead wives.

Ida responded to this need by training to be a doctor. She returned to India, not only to serve as a doctor, but later began a hospital and established a medical school. It is reported that on one occasion, a letter was simply addressed: Dr. Ida Scudder, India. She received it because she was so well known. God calls some to cross the world with the good news. (Lights orange or red candle from flame of white candle.) I light this candle in honor of those who are carrying the Light of Life to people walking in darkness all across the world.

(Exit speaker 3.)

Reader: "For mine eyes have seen thy salvation/which thou hast prepared in the presence of all peoples,/a light for revelation to the Gentiles,/and for glory to thy people Israel" (Luke 2:30-32, RSV).

Choir sings: "Here Is My Life"

Leader: It is said that Susanna Wesley was a woman of prayer. Her husband was a minister, and they were poor. Susanna had nineteen children. Her most famous children were the founders of Methodism, John and Charles. Susanna prayed daily with her children and in her personal closet. She gave individual religious instruction to her children every week. When John and Charles were still young, they witnessed in prisons, gave money to the poor, and belonged to prayer groups. John was called "the parson of the saddlebags" because he traveled so many miles on horseback to preach the gospel.

(Enter speaker 4.)

Speaker 4: Jesus assures his followers that he will go with them. If young people are to be effective witnesses, they must discipline themselves to daily prayer. As a young boy planning to be a mechanic, Bill Wallace felt God calling him to the mission field. He was reading his Bible and surrendered to God as his servant.

After much studying and preparation, Bill Wallace went to China as a missionary doctor. When the Communists took over, they planted a gun under his mattress and accused him of being a spy. He died in a Communist prison. Followers of Dr. Wallace risked punishment themselves to place a marker on his grave which said, "For me to live is Christ."

(Exit speaker 4.)

Choir sings: "Fill My Cup, Lord," page 68.

(Enter speaker 5.)

Speaker 5: When young people have limitations and handicaps, they sometimes feel God ought to excuse them from serving. Mary Slessor grew up in a home with an alcoholic father; but when God called her to Africa, she said, "Here am I. I will go." Mary worked among warring tribes of heathen people who came to know God's love through her.

Martin Luther grew up in an atmosphere where he learned to fear God. He used to get on his knees and confess his sins for six hours at a time, so afraid was he that God would punish him. As Luther studied the New Testament, the truth that he was saved by grace through faith freed him. He accepted God's forgiveness; but all through Luther's life he was, at times, overcome by deep depression.

In spite of depression and a problem with insomnia, Luther stood firm against hypocrisy and false teaching. This meant that he defied the church leaders of his day. He was harassed and imprisoned, but Luther's stand against the church hierarchy was a key force in the Protestant Reformation. (Lights green candle from white one.) I light this candle to encourage us to dedicate our limitations to God. He can give us victory.

(Exit speaker 5.)

Reader: The apostle Paul said, "And to keep me from being too elated by the abundance of revelations, a thorn was given me in the flesh, a messenger of Satan, to harass me, to keep me from being too elated. Three times I besought the Lord about this, that it should leave me; but he said to me, 'My grace is sufficient for you, for my power is made perfect in weakness.' I will all the more gladly boast of my weaknesses, . . . insults, hardships, persecutions, and calamities; for when I am weak, then I am strong" (2 Cor. 12:7-10, RSV).

Choir sings: "His Way, Mine," page 83.

(Enter speaker 6.)

Speaker 6: If young people are to live for Christ, they must be courageous. It is not popular to be a Christian. In fact, it never has been popular. Jesus told his disciples to expect to be ridiculed and persecuted.

We are told that many Christians are suffering today behind the Iron Curtain in atheistic Communist–controlled countries. A missionary to the Communist countries calls himself Brother Andrew. He has discovered little bands of Christians all over the Communist world. In Russia a pastor pulled him aside and showed him his distorted fingernails, the results of torture in prison. In Czechoslovakia, a Christian gave him a tiny cup and said, "This is a symbol of the cup of suffering we are being forced to drink." Everywhere Bibles are scarce, and Brother Andrew has risked his life to get Bibles to these people.

In a small town called Macedonia in Yugoslavia, Brother Andrew was to speak to a little group of Christians. He kept asking the pastor if they shouldn't be heading for the meeting place. Each time the pastor said that it was not quite time.

Finally, the pastor took Brother Andrew to the window. "Now it is time," he said. All across the fields the people were coming by twos and threes, carrying their lanterns. It was safer to gather after dark and to come slowly in very small groups. Brother Andrew said such little groups of folks with lanterns, headed for a secret place of worship, became familiar in the Communist world. Some carry the light of faith amid great suffering.

What of us? Do we draw back from owning Christ openly? Do we take up habits that dishonor him, just to please other teenagers? (Lights green candle from white one.) I light this candle in honor of those who suffer in his name everywhere and as a reminder that being his followers should cost something.

(Exit speaker 6.)

Choir sings: "When I Think of the Cross," page 72.

(Arrangements should be made ahead of time for the six speakers to pick up the candles they lighted and march out to direct all the congregation to make a big circle around the room. As this is done, the choir will sing, over and over, "Shine," p. 50, and "Hold Out Your Light," p. 86. When everyone is settled, the Leader speaks. Reader should have candle and stand beside the Leader.)

Leader: "Again Jesus spoke to them, saying, 'I am the light of the world; he who follows me will not walk in darkness, but will have the light of life'" (John 8:12, RSV). Because I have accepted Christ as my Savior, his light has entered my life to dispel the darkness. (She picks up center candle on table.) I am letting this candle represent my life. I light the candle of the one who stands beside me. (She lights the candle of the one standing beside her.) As we pass the light around the room, we symbolize the fact that we will not keep the light of salvation to ourselves, but we will pass it on.

Choir sings: "Pass It On," page 60, as the candles are lighted.

(If it takes too long to pass one light, one by one, all the way around the room, have the six speakers to light a few candles between. This will speed things up.)

Leader: This dark room has become filled with light. This is a good reminder of the darkness in our world. Approximately two-thirds of the world's population do not know Christ as Savior.

Reader: "You are the light of the world. A city set on a hill cannot be hid. Nor do men light a lamp and put it under a bushel, but on a stand, and it gives light to all in the house. Let your light so shine before men, that they may see your good works and give glory to your Father who is in heaven" (Matt. 5:14-16, RSV).

Leader: Now, as we leave this room carrying our lighted candles, may we go with determination to carry the light of Christ across the street, across the state, and around the world. As we go, let us sing over and over the first verse of "Send the Light" (p. 304 in the 1975 *Baptist Hymnal*). (Exit out various doors, directed by the six speakers.)

Drama 3: "If You Do It Unto the Least"

General instructions for presenting "If You Do It Unto the Least":

1. Have the participants memorize the parts. Practice at least three times and stress speaking out with enthusiasm!

2. For staging, ferns may be placed across the front or on either side. Have the narrator stand up front to read. Let choir sit down front or on stage to the back. Other staging is left to you.

3. Suggestions for dress and characterization:

A. Materially Needy—all barefooted and poorly dressed

B. Juvenile Delinquents

1. In tight jeans, with lots of makeup and long earrings if female; leather jacket and boots if male; with a very sarcastic attitude.

2. Similar to No. 1.

3. Let a girl wear pants, long beads, and a maternity shirt; lots of eye makeup; sour, sarcastic attitude.

C. Those Without Christ

1. Should look like a man from the Near East or Israel. A headband, slacks, a silky jacket and turban would be appropriate—or hair wrapped in scarf. He needs to bring out a small rug or large colorful towel, kneel down on it, and bow his face to the ground five times.

2. Preferably a black-haired girl wearing her hair straight, dressed in any Oriental kimono or dress with slides for shoes. Have her bow, as in worship, folding her hands and moving lips, as if praying.

3. A Black person should do this part. The person should bring out a wooden doll, place it on the floor, and bow before it.

4. Several Americans dressed in dinner dresses with lots of jewelry, males in dinner jackets, carrying cocktail glasses, dancing, laughing, etc.

5. Have a male come out in a doctor's jacket with a thermometer. Have a patient coming who has his temperature taken.

6. A male with a suit, wearing glasses, comes out with a large book.

7. A male pretending to smoke marijuana cigarette, wearing jeans.

D. Physically Sick

1. Someone rolls a male in wheelchair on-stage; he is dressed in pajamas and housecoat.

2. A male wears dark glasses and carries cane as he finds way across stage.

3. Two people enter dressed in ordinary clothes. They are using sign language with each other.

4. Every part, including music, should

move along steadily, with no gaps, unless waiting for person acting out a part to get offstage and next one onstage.

5. Have good lighting and use microphone (and everyone needs to practice using it). At least, the narrator should have a microphone if more are not available.

6. The choir may wear robes. Select the best choir director and pianist you can find. Some guitarists would be effective. I suggest you buy copies of *Sing 'N' Celebrate*.

If You Do It Unto the Least

(A play for teenagers, depicting human need)

(Enter Materially Needy 1.)

Materially Needy 1: I am the materially needy, hungry people found in every nation, found in streets all over the world. My stomach is empty; my eyes are bulging! I never know what it means to go to bed full and satisfied.

(Enter Materially Needy 2.)

Materially Needy 2: I am more than half of all the people of the world and I go to bed hungry every night. To whom do I speak? I speak to you who have never really known hunger. You say, "I'm about to starve! I surely am hungry." But you have never missed having three meals a day. Sometimes you complain because you don't like liver or beans, but I tell you I eat out of garbage cans on the streets. You say I'm exaggerating? Oh, no I'm not!

(Enter Materially Needy 3.)

Materially Needy 3: Would that you would lift up your eyes and see! You are saying, "What can I do? It's too bad about you, but I don't have enough to help even a few of you millions of hungry people." You say you are sorry some of us in Latin America actually live on the streets because we have no houses in which to live.

(Enter Materially Needy 4.)

Materially Needy 4: I am the poor lady a missionary to Brazil told you church members about. You remember that I got on a bus with my baby wrapped in a small blanket in my arms. It was cold and I wanted to ride the bus. But when the conductor discovered I didn't have the few pennies to pay to ride, he put me off. However, some kind people on the bus persuaded the driver to let me back on, and I rode to town. When I got off, the missionary handed me a little money out the window. I moved on up to a store doorway, lay down on the sidewalk with my baby, and prepared to sleep for the night; for you see, I have no home!

(Enter Materially Needy 5.)

Materially Needy 5: You wish you lived in a nicer neighborhood. You're anxious to keep up with the Joneses, must have a new car, and must be as well dressed as all the fashionable people of today! I have no decent clothes and no feeling of belonging and worth. I am sick, weak, discouraged! Will no one hear my plea? What can *you* do? You can share as God commanded. You can carefully give God his tithe; but more, you can give whenever you see the need beyond the tithe!

Narrator: The hungry need to be fed. The thirsty need drink. The homeless need shelter. God speaks to the materially rich and says, "Every one to whom much is given, of him will much be required; and of him to whom men commit much they will demand the more" (Luke 12:48b, RSV). (Exit Materially Needy.)

Choir sings: "O God, We Pray for All Mankind" or "Where Cross the Crowded Ways of Life" or "It's Our World"

(Enter Juvenile Delinquent 1.)

Juvenile Delinquent 1: I am the countless juvenile delinquents, turning early to the road of crime, distrusting others, and finding that I am mistrusted and condemned. You would condemn us? You say it's a crime and a sin to steal, to kill, to destroy the property of others? Oh, but often I have never been taught what is right. I have lived in crowded, slum sections of town all my life. I have been commanded by parents who seem to know nothing of love. I have gone to school with people who have nice clothes and cars, live in comfortable homes—kids who are accepted, who rate with the other fellows and girls! I can't make friends because I'm not like the other kids!

(Enter Juvenile Delinquent 2.)

Juvenile Delinquent 2: I'm looked down on. What if I do steal a car? At least I get a thrill out of it. I have no place to play, except in the streets. You think it is a disgrace I run around on the streets with a bunch of tough guys? Well, you don't have to approve, society! I owe you nothing. At least, these guys are my friends and we think of some mighty interesting jobs to pull.

(Enter Juvenile Delinquent 3.)

Juvenile Delinquent 3: Yes, I'm those unwed mothers everybody scoffs at, but I have never been loved. At least, somebody showed me some attention. You remind me that my body is the temple of God and the Bible says I should keep it holy. Well, that is a noble thought! But I hunger and long to be loved! Nobody seems to care if I live or die. Somebody needs to care. My rich parents don't care!

Narrator: What can *you* do? You can try to help these neglected young people. It would be wonderful if somebody could just love them for what they are, could take an interest in them and help them to find their place in this world. They feel lonely and often in despair. If you have skills, knowledge, and most of all, love, you can help them. I know you can!

Choir sings: "The Light of God Is Falling" or "Here Is My Life" (Exit Juvenile Delinquents.)

(Enter Those Without Christ 1.)

Those Without Christ 1: I do not know any Savior named Jesus Christ! He was only a prophet. Every day five times daily I bow toward Mecca and say, "Allah is the one God and Mohammed is his prophet." Daily I say my prayers. There is a hunger deep in my heart to find someone on whom I can depend. Even my closest friends and family do not always understand me, and many times they are unable to help me when I have problems. I cry out in my prayers to one who does not respond. It is as though he did not hear, for I never feel that my needs are answered. Never do my prayers bring peace, though I cry out day and night!

(Enter Those Without Christ 2.)

Those Without Christ 2: I am the millions of Oriental people who bow before the placid, plump figure of Buddha as the gong sounds.

(Enter Those Without Christ 3.)

Those Without Christ 3: I am Africa's hordes placing little bits of food before wooden idols, ever and anon coming to appease the wrath of evil spirits. My life is ridden with fear. Evil is all around me. I must pay my vows to my gods, or some awful thing may befall me. My idols never answer the deep yearning of my heart. I wonder, can they hear?

(Enter Those Without Christ 4.)

Those Without Christ 4: I am the wild, materialistic throngs of Americans, feeding myself on the sinful pleasures that fade as a bubble. Nights are spent in wild reveling, the alcohol bottle my constant companion. My lusts never go unsatisfied; in selfishness and greed I defy my body and that of others. In business I take what I want from others every chance I get. You've got to take advantage of others before they have a chance to take advantage of you.

(Enter Those Without Christ 5.)

Those Without Christ 5: I am the professional man who knows how to take a shortcut, the doctor who runs patients through the office as fast as I can, with little real concern for how they feel or what their real infirmities are. Well, yes, I could take a little more time, be a little more sympathetic. But, after all, I've got to make a living—buy a summer home, a boat, and take trips abroad. Well, you just can't have all the compassion for a patient that people are always yapping about. You've got to be practical.

(Enter Those Without Christ 6.)

Those Without Christ 6: I'm the intellectual snob who knows a real man is his own God. My mind is the most important thing to me. God, what God? Why, I can get along fine. I am a mature person, self-sufficient. What do I need with God?

(Enter Those Without Christ 7.)

Those Without Christ 7: I am a young person who believes in hanging loose. Adults are so uptight and always on somebody's case! So, my friends and I like to get high. What's wrong with a little "grass" now and then? We don't shoot up or nothin'! But being one of the crowd is what counts with me!

Narrator: These represent many needs, and they are all crying with multitoned voices. Though they do not realize their need, any little moment they stop their pace, they feel empty and deeply lonely. They aren't truly happy. Sometimes they put on an artificial smile; but if you look deep into their eyes, you will see they are unhappy. What can *you* do? You can preach Christ day and night. You must live him and love him, reflect him in word, in action, in impulse, and in every conduct.

Choir sings: "Rise Up, O Men of God" or "Hark, the Voice of Jesus Calling" or "Reach Out and Touch"

(Exit Those Without Christ; Enter Physically Sick 1.)

Physically Sick 1: I am the physically sick and impaired, sitting in wheelchairs, lying on beds. I long to do things for myself, to be free to get up and walk out into God's beautiful world. It has been so long since I have been without pain. I cannot remember what it feels like to know relief and comfort. Nagging pain, sleepless nights with fever, and restless longing to be able to rest are all mine.

(Enter Physically Sick 2.)

Physically Sick 2: I am the blind, those who cannot enjoy the beauty of a blue sky with soft, fluffy white clouds; red, blue, brown birds; little soft brown chipmunks; dainty little purple flowers; numerous yellow jonquils; blossoming peach trees. I never have seen the grandeur of a mountain reaching up toward heaven. Can you imagine the fact that I have never seen a big silvery moon or the glory of a sky studded with diamond-sparkling stars? Can you understand anyone who has never seen a human face or looked into soft eyes or at glossy hair? People I come in contact with make me wonder so often how they look, but I am never able to see them.

(Enter Physically Sick 3.)

Physically Sick 3: I am the deaf who have never been awakened by the chatter of noisy birds. I have never heard a human voice or the chords of a piano. The gorgeous strains of Handel's *Messiah* have never brought a response from me, for such music has fallen on stopped ears. "The Love of God" and "The Lord's Prayer" have never been sung so I could hear them.

Choir sings: "O Jesus, Master, When Today," or "The Greatest Gift"

Narrator: Reads Matthew 25:34-45.

Choir sings: "The Master Hath Come" or "Shine"

Drama 4: Stable Bows and Living Arrows

This is a play that presents the struggle of one particular teenager to decide between the guidance of her parents and the pull of her peers. It depicts the complex adjustment of parents who want to allow adequate freedom but are torn by anxiety over the consequences a child might face in making poor decisions.

The play closes with a new understanding by the mother for the rights of her daughter and a new respect on the part of the daughter for the protection her parents have provided.

The play could be effectively used at a program emphasizing teen-adult understanding. It could be followed by discussion or used as the closing inspirational part of the program. It could be presented as a Sunday School assembly program or even at a parent-teen banquet.

Characters: Beth, a teenage girl in the eleventh grade at school

Barbara, another teenage girl in the eleventh grade at school

Mrs. Bailey, Beth's mother

Mrs. Taylor, a friend

Scene 1: The setting is a living room in the Bailey home.

(As the scene opens, Mrs. Bailey is dressed for church and is in the living room. Beth is offstage in her bedroom.)

Mother: Beth, come on! We'll be late for Sunday School!

Beth: Just go on. I'll come on to church later.

Mother: We've been through this before. As long as you live in this house, you will go to Sunday School and church every Sunday you aren't sick.

Beth: Oh, I forgot to tell you. I'm sick!

Mother: You know very well that's made up.

Beth: It certainly is not! I'm sick—sick of Sunday School and church, sick enough to throw up!

(She makes an angry flurry into the room, ready for Sunday School.)

Mother: Where is your Bible?

Beth: I couldn't find it.

Mother: I can't believe you are a junior in high school. You act much younger.

Beth: No wonder I act younger. You and Daddy police me around like I was three years old. Other friends my age don't go to Sunday School unless they want to go. They are treated like the adults they are.

Mother: Hurry! Daddy's waiting in the car.

(Exit and curtain closes.)

Scene 2: The setting is a bench somewhere on the way home from school. Beth and Barbara have on school clothes and are carrying a few books. They come in and sit down on the bench.

Beth: I've been wanting to talk to you, Barbara.

Barbara: What about?

Beth: I just want to know how you got your parents to stop babying you. Mine still make me go to Sunday School and church and oversee everything I do. They are unbelievably old-fashioned.

Barbara: Oh, my brother and I have always had freedom. My parents never have gone to church. They are too intellectual for that kind of stuff. Ever since we were little, Mother has said we were given minds of our own so we could learn to choose.

Beth: What time do you come in from a date?

(Barbara laughs.)

Barbara: Sometimes I don't.

Beth: You mean you stay out all night?

Barbara: If I want to, because my parents never wait up for me.

Beth: Where do you go on your dates?

Barbara: Well, there's a night spot about ten miles out of town where a group of us go. We dance and fool around. It's super! Why don't you go with us this Saturday night? I could fix you up with a cute guy.

Beth: Are you joking? My mother would never allow that.

Barbara: Oh, use your head! We could plan it out carefully. Tell your mother I've invited you to spend the night with me at my house. The guys can meet us at my place. We can stay out as late as we like, and your mother won't know the difference.

Beth: Uh—well, I don't know.

Barbara: Hey, you aren't scared, are you?

Beth: No.

Barbara: Well, it's set then. Why don't we stop at the pay phone down the street and let you call your mother?

Beth: OK.

(They go to phone and Beth picks up receiver and dials her mother.)

Beth: Hello, Mom. Barbara has asked me to spend Friday night with her. I could take my clothes to school and go home with her from there. We may go to a show, but I'll be back by lunchtime Saturday.

Mother: Barbara who?

Beth: Oh, Mother, Barbara Black, of course!

Mother: I didn't realize you were even good friends. How well do you know her?

Beth: Mother, just say yes. You always make a simple request into a major court decision! It's unbelievable!

Mother: Well, I guess it'll be all right this time.

Beth: Thanks. See you in a few minutes. I'm on the way home. Bye.

Mother: Bye.

Beth (turning to Barbara): She agreed.

Barbara: Great, man, great! We'll have a blast!

(Exit and curtain closes.)

Scene 3: Setting is a nightclub or nightspot. (This part can be completely omitted, except for the narration, if you like.) Have a group of loud teens laughing and talking to each other, smoking, drinking, dancing, sitting on each other's laps and acting drunk. Among the teens are Beth and Barbara. (If you just use narration, the atmosphere could be created by some loud teen noises offstage.)

Narrator: So Barbara urged Beth to go with her to her favorite hangout, the Purple Onion. Beth drank because the kids pushed and called her names when she said she did not drink. She smoked grass for the first time because everybody else was smoking it. It was 2 AM when the girls got home, and it would have been later, but Beth made a scene when the guy she had just met tried to force her to have intercourse. She cried so hysterically Barbara told the boys to take them home.

(Curtain closes.)

Scene 4: Living room of the Bailey home.

Narrator: Meanwhile, in the home of Mr. and Mrs. Bailey, a Christian friend, Mrs. Taylor, is visiting Mrs. Bailey.

Mrs. Bailey: Eleanor, I asked you to come tonight while my husband John has gone bowling with his league because I feel I need you to pray with me.

Mrs. Taylor: You know I'm happy to do so, Joyce, but what seems to be the trouble?

Mrs. Bailey: I'm worried about Beth. She has been rebelling against Sunday School and church this entire year. She keeps saying we baby her and wanting more freedom. Tonight she is spending the night with a girl who does not have a very good reputation, the best I can tell. I just couldn't say no again. You raised two lovely daughters. How did you do it?

Mrs. Taylor: Well, we surely had our ups and downs.

Mrs. Bailey: Was there ever a time your girls refused to go to church?

Mrs. Taylor: I remember a time when Peggy, our youngest, said she didn't get a thing out of church. We talked it over. My husband and I prayed about it every day, and we said she could visit different churches on Sunday nights. She could compare these. We asked her to pray that God would lead her in her choosing.

Mrs. Bailey: Did she visit other Baptist churches or other denominations?

Mrs. Taylor: Both. We asked her just to keep us informed and let us know what she thought. In fact, we agreed to visit with her once in a while, if she wished.

Mrs. Bailey: How did it work out?

Mrs. Taylor: It was months before we could even begin to see what the outcome might be. My husband and I tried never to act frightened, rigid, or dogmatic. When Peggy said critical things about Baptists and positive things about Episcopalians or Catholics, we honestly tried to see the good points with an open mind.

Mrs. Bailey: I'm sure Beth already feels we are dogmatic. That's why she's so rebellious, I guess. And I'm sure she can sense our fear.

Mrs. Taylor: We, as parents, can be threatened easily when it comes to our children and what we feel is good for them. Of course, my husband and I grew up in the Baptist church. We had to keep reminding ourselves we *did* have a rather narrow exposure and the Baptists do not have the only corner on truth.

Mrs. Bailey: I know what you mean. John and I also grew up in Baptist homes and have always been so active that we just can't stand to think of Beth belonging to any other church.

Mrs. Taylor: The thing is that in our enthusiasm for our beliefs, we can be more devoted to being Baptists than being Christian, sometimes. Truth is a broad and tremendous thing. Surely God is not honored by our unwillingness to allow our children an honest search for truth. Also, a vote of confidence in our children at their time of searching for truth will support them when they actually do need support.

Mrs. Bailey: I guess I never thought of things as you have presented them. Truth is broad, and I've acted so very narrow. And I know Beth feels I don't trust her. I surely haven't given support.

Mrs. Taylor: God has chosen humans to be parents. That means we do make mistakes. But one thing that often opened channels between Peggy and me, as well as my other daughter, was for me to be able to see where I was wrong. It seemed that when I could say, "I'm sorry. I was wrong" that brought me closer to my daughters than anything.

Mrs. Bailey: I can't remember when I've ever said that to Beth. I've felt that would make me appear weak and inadequate.

Mrs. Taylor: I used to feel that way. But our children know we are human. They live with us each day, so they see our weaknesses. When we admit them, they have more respect for us. They also know they aren't perfect, so there is an identification and understanding we miss when we try to appear perfect.

Mrs. Bailey: That makes lots of sense.

Mrs. Taylor: Well, my dear, shall we open our hearts to our Heavenly Father in special prayer for Beth?

Mrs. Bailey: Yes.

(They bow their heads and the curtain closes.)

Narrator: So Mrs. Taylor and Mrs. Bailey prayed that Beth would be blessed by God's presence and guidance. They prayed that Mr. and Mrs. Bailey would have more wisdom in dealing with Beth. They prayed earnestly for fifteen or twenty minutes. The Bible says, "Pray constantly, give thanks in all circumstances; for this is the will of God in Christ Jesus for you." "Therefore confess your sins to one another, and pray for one another, that you may be healed. The prayer of a righteous man has great power in its effects." "Likewise the Spirit helps us in our weakness; for we do not know how to pray as we ought, but the Spirit himself intercedes for us with sighs too deep for words" (1 Thess. 5:17-18; Jas. 5:16; Rom. 8:26, RSV).

Scene 5: The setting is the living room of the Bailey home. Mrs. Bailey is reading the paper. Beth enters, obviously depressed.

Mother: Well, hi! I didn't expect you for several hours.

Beth: I know, but I decided there was lots I needed to get done this morning.

Mother: Well, how was your overnight?

Beth: Oh, fine.

Mother: Did you go to a movie?

Beth: No, we just stayed home and watched TV.

Mother: I see. Well, you'll have to invite Barbara over for a meal sometime. Your father and I want to get to know her.

Beth: Well, maybe we can. (Looks down and seems even more depressed.)

Mother: Beth, are you not feeling well? You don't seem like yourself this morning. (There is a pause as Beth looks down.)

Beth: Oh, Mother, I feel awful! I've been dishonest with you about everything.

Mother: What do you mean?

Beth: Yesterday I talked to Barbara after school. She said she goes out to a nightclub when she dates. She wanted me to go. I told her I couldn't. She said we could just tell you I was going to spend the night with her, and she would get me a date. Then we'd go to the Purple Onion.

Mother: And that's what you did?

Beth: Yes, and it was awful! Everybody was drinking and smoking grass. They pushed me to join in and acted like I was off when I said no, so I finally did drink some and smoke a little. (Begins to cry.) I feel so ashamed! I've let you and Daddy down!

(Mrs. Bailey comes over to Beth and puts her arms around her.)

Beth: Then, Mother, this boy I had just met kept trying to force himself on me. I got so hysterical that Barbara finally told the boys to take us home about 2 AM.

Mother: I'm sorry you had to have such a frightening experience. But it sounds like you learned a great deal.

Beth: You don't hate me?

Mother: No, dear. I don't hate you. We all make mistakes. I've realized that your father and I have also been wrong. (They sit down together.)

Beth: What do you mean?

Mother: We've been too anxious to try to force our views and beliefs on you. We've forgotten that a child cannot inherit faith or truth. The child must think, question, and search to carve out his own faith in the midst of his unfolding life. We've been afraid and anxious. Therefore, we haven't given you the trust and support, or even the freedom, to develop your own philosophy of life. Your father and I have acted like we have all the answers, which we don't. It has been natural for you to rebel.

(Beth cries and hugs her mother.)

Beth: Oh, Mother, I do love you and Daddy!

Mother: I know you do, and we are so thankful that you are our daughter. When your father gets home, we want to sit down with you and talk out our conflicts and ways we can be more helpful to you and allow you more choices. After all, we can't always follow you around and tell you what to do. Would it fit into your plans for all of us to talk together right after lunch today?

Beth: Sure. (They look at each other and smile. Beth gets up to leave.) I need to go clean my room before lunch.

Mother: Fine.

(Curtain closes.)

(Narrator may read the section "On Children" from *The Prophet* by Kahlil Gibran.)

Drama 5: More Valuable than Birds

Use: This skit can be used at a banquet or for outdoor morning devotions. It should involve lightness and humor as well as instruction and inspiration.

Characters: Eight people with some feathers, construction paper cut as feathers, or whatever can be used to give the coloring of the different birds represented, each with a strip of paper hung around the neck containing the name of the bird he represents. Look up these birds in a book that pictures them in color:

1. Mockingbird
2. Woodpecker
3. Cedar Waxwing
4. Cowbird
5. Mourning Dove
6. Chimney Swift
7. Tanager
8. Killdeer

A narrator should be chosen who will speak out very clearly and enthusiastically. You might need to use a public address system. Be sure the narrator practices using it with someone who knows how to operate it. Have a pianist and other instrumentalist, plus a soloist, to help with the program. The piano, the flute, and a good soloist can do a beautiful job on "Flee as a Bird," in *The Broadman Hymnal.* Throughout the presentation the instrumentalists could play songs such as "Mockingbird Hill," "Bye-Bye Blackbird," "Bluebird of Happiness," and "Woody Woodpecker."

Setting: A scene in the woods. Some department store in town may have plastic greenery and artificial flowers you can use to decorate. You could paint a backdrop with trees and grass, or cut limbs and pinecones you could place around for atmosphere.

Narrator: Greetings, ladies and gentlemen! I am here to introduce a special presentation on birds. First, we will have (names of musicians) to entertain us with "Feed the Birds," from the musical *Mary Poppins.*

(Musicians perform "Feed the Birds.")

(Enter Mockingbird.)

Narrator: Now, this is one bird that may be very familiar to all of us—the mockingbird. I guess we all know that it's hard to determine when we are hearing a mockingbird. He is such a copycat. He can imitate the song of the sparrow, the meow of a cat, or the creak of an iron gate. Mockingbirds remind me of some people I know. You never know what they think. They repeat the views of popular people. They take up the habits of others. You never know what they believe or if they have any standards of their own. Oh, how the world needs fewer mockingbirds!

(Enter Woodpecker.)

Narrator: We've all seen woodpeckers pecking on trees. We can see rows of holes where they've pecked in search of insects and grubs. Do you know how a woodpecker gets the grubs out of the tree? He pecks a hole and pulls it out with his tongue. The woodpecker's tongue is twice as long as his head. (The person who is Woodpecker should pull out bubble gum or a piece of red balloon from his mouth.) A woodpecker's long tongue reminds me of some people I know who spend most of their time criticizing and gossiping about others. Of course, such activity is a dead giveaway that such a person is insecure.

(Enter Cedar Waxwing.)

Narrator: This is a beautiful cedar waxwing. This bird could be called the Lone Ranger of birds because there are black circles around his eyes that look like a mask. He is gray with a tail spotted with yellow, red, and white. Cedar waxwings love berries. You may have seen them pluck berries and pass them down to share with other members of the flock. Such a gesture of sharing needs to be repeated all over the world. More than one-half of the people of the world go to bed hungry every night. In America we spend more than twice as much for alcoholic beverages as we give to all religious causes. Evidently we haven't learned yet that, as Jesus said, "It is more blessed to give than to receive" (Acts 20:35*b*).

(Enter Cowbird.)

Narrator: The cowbird has a brown head and a black body. The oddest thing about this bird is the way the mother will not build her own nest or care for her young. Instead, she drops her eggs into another bird's nest. For example, sometimes it is the mother bluebird who winds up feeding the baby cowbirds. Since the bluebirds are so much smaller than the cowbirds, the baby cowbirds often get all the food and the bluebirds starve to death. This kind of irresponsibility reminds me of some people I know who take on all kinds of jobs and think nothing of not doing them. Sometimes others wind up carrying a double load.

(Exit Mockingbird, Woodpecker, Cedar Waxwing, and Cowbird. Enter Chimney Swift.)

Narrator: The chimney swift lives inside chimneys. He makes a little nest that looks like half of a tea cup. Do you know how he attaches this nest to the inside of a chimney? He uses his saliva.

(Enter Tanager.)

Narrator: Tanagers are interesting birds. There are summer tanagers and scarlet tanagers. The male scarlet tanager has essentially the same coloring as the summer tanager, except that his wings are black. The male is a bright red and the female is greenish-yellow. The strange thing about tanagers is that they are ventriloquists. You may hear a sound and look in the direction of the sound but see no bird. After studying the situation, you will discover that the tanager has thrown his voice in a direction other than his location so he will not be detected.

(Enter Killdeer.)

Narrator: Some birds, such as the killdeer, are quite tricky. A mother may see a person coming toward the nest where her young are living. She will squawk loudly as she moves away from her nesting area right on the ground. She drags her wing as though hurt. Such action is a decoy. When the hunter comes near her, she lifts herself off the ground and flies away.

(Enter Mourning Dove.)

Narrator: God has designed birds with amazing intricacy and wisdom. There's the mourning dove, who usually eats hard seeds. Because God knew the baby mourning dove could not digest the seeds, he put into the mother's body a special gland. When the mother has babies, this special gland produces a soft, cheesy substance she pumps into the baby's mouth when he is hungry.

(Exit Mourning Dove, Chimney Swift, Tanager, Killdeer.)

Narrator: Birds are fascinating creatures. What care God used in designing them! How unique they are! Jesus said, "Are not two sparrows sold for a penny? And not one of them will fall to the ground without your Father's will. But even the hairs of your head are all numbered. Fear not, therefore; you are of more value than many sparrows" (Matt. 10:29-31, RSV). If God created birds with such care, how wise we would be to place our lives in his hands for direction and care! Isaiah said, "Therefore the Lord waits to be gracious to you;/therefore he exalts himself to show mercy to you./For the Lord is a God of justice;/blessed are all those who wait for Him" (Isa. 30:18, RSV).

"Flee as a Bird," by soloist, piano, and flute, will conclude skit.

14
Camp Program Ideas

In my fifteen years of directing camp, I learned that "variety is the spice of life," and it is also the spur that keeps camp enthusiasm alive. I am writing some of the activities our campers and staffers enjoyed. These may give new ideas to those who are planning and directing camp. They may also be adapted for youth programming in a church.

Indoor Fair

One of the most helpful rainy-day activities is an indoor fair. You will need a large room—a gym, auditorium, or the like—and a stage with a curtain and one or two other rooms or areas. If you use an auditorium with a porch, you can put tubs of water with apples in them on the porch so people can bob for apples. If there are rafters, hang some apples from these on strong string so that people can also bob for apples on strings.

In one corner of the auditorium draw off a cake walk, numbering the squares. Set up a record player, and have little individual cakes or cookies you can give to the person standing on the chosen number when the music stops.

Along the sides of the room, have some contests and give penny candy to the winners. Place some soft-drink bottles in a line and give the participants ten dried beans. If a person gets three of the ten beans in the bottle, give him some candy. Place blown-up balloons on a wooden board. You could put nails into the board and tie the balloons to these. Give people three darts to throw at the balloons and give candy to those who pop five. Place some lighted candles in a row and let contestants shoot at them with water pistols. Those who put out the flame are winners. You could also arrange a variation of "Pin the Tail on the Donkey," using a drawing some talented staffer could make of a clown whose nose people place on his face

while blindfolded. Put up some card tables and have a bingo game going on. Give the winners penny candy.

Cut construction paper in the shape of fish. Write out fortunes on each fish, such as: "You will grow up to be a great musician" or "When you get home, there will be an unusual letter waiting for you." You could also write fortunes about staffers everybody knows, such as: "Ask the waterfront director about that special person she gets lots of mail from" or "Find out what staffer is a good mechanic." Make enough fish so every person will get one. You could use several regular fishing poles or sticks with strings and a pin at the end. Prop these against the piano or a large table or two turned sideways. Have several staffers behind the piano or tables to place the fish onto the hooks or pins.

On the stage, or in a separate room, have a side show. This could include a playpen made out of a huge cardboard box. A small staff member could be dressed like a baby, sucking a bottle, and crying. The sign on the box could say: The World's Largest Infant. Hang a sheet so that a person's head is stuck through it. Maybe it would be best to put the person doing this part into a big box and cover it with a sheet with a hole in it. The person would stick his head through the box. There should be lots of catsup on the sheet and floor and a sign saying: The Human Without a Body. Two persons about the same size and coloring could be wrapped in a blanket and marked: Siamese Twins. One person could be dressed like the Fat Lady, with pillows stuffed under her clothes.

In a separate room, set up a horror house. Have lots of screaming. Blindfold each child as he is brought in and tell him he is to guess what part of the body he is feeling. (Separate dishes will hold the items.) Let grapes be the eyes, chicken liver the person's liver, noodles the intestines, and the like. Be sure the room is dark. You could pop a balloon once in a while and even have some things hanging from the ceiling.

Several people should be dressed as clowns and be running around acting silly. You could arrange to have a pinata hanging from the ceiling. It should be made around a large brown bag base and be filled with enough candy for everybody attending the fair. You could close everything and let people take turns being blindfolded and hitting at the pinata until the candy falls out. Use a broom handle, or the like, for hitting; be sure everyone stays back out of the way of the one hitting. Strips of colorful paper could be cut and glued over the bag. If someone knows how to make the face of a particular animal, such as a donkey, that would make the pinata attractive.

Olympics

If this is a camp event, each cabin will need to elect competitors for each event. Each cabin will also need a flagbearer, if you have world flags that can be carried in a flag ceremony. Ahead of the actual Olympics, there needs to be a practice for all those carrying flags and a practice for all those competing in events. Events could include the high jump, hurdles, broad jump, a softball throw (instead of javelin throw), and a relay event.

To begin the Olympics, the spectators should gather on the grounds where the events will begin. If there is a hill leading down to the athletic field, it looks good to have the flagbearers and competitors march down the hill. At any rate, some distance from the spectators, a torchbearer should lead the line. You can make a torch of construction paper and have red crepe paper sticking up to look like a flame. Then persons carrying the American and Christian flags should march, side by side, behind the torchbearer. Half of the competitors will march behind the Christian flag and half behind the American flag. The flag of a different country will be assigned to each cabin and be carried by their flagbearer. Behind this flag will march the competitors from that cabin. This group should march onto the field, and someone should lead a salute to the American flag and the Christian flag. Then the events begin.

For the high jump, you will need two heavy square boards with nails, exactly opposite, driven up each board. A cane can be used across the nails. It is moved up each time the jumpers begin to jump again. As people touch the cane, they are eliminated. Sawdust can be used for the campers to jump into.

The person in charge of Olympics needs lots of helpers who know ahead of time what to do. For example, they should keep records on which cabins

win each event. Also, they can spot in the races.

The hurdles are made by sticking small rows of sticks into the ground, each with a nail about midway. Across each are canes. As many as six rows of hurdles can be lined up. If persons in more than six cabins are competing, they can be divided into more than one race, with winners of each competing again. You need spotters at the end of the run to hold a cord and watch to see who is first, second, and third.

The broad jump involves a flat board pushed down even with the ground. Those competing run, jump onto the board, and spring from it. A mechanical measuring tape can be used to measure each jump. These should be recorded. If a person's foot goes over the board when he jumps, this jump does not count. However, each competitor should be allowed two jumps, with the best jump being counted toward first-, second-, and third-place winners.

In the softball throw, the counselor of each cabin, if this is a camp setting, can stand where the ball fell. The point is to see who can throw a ball the greatest distance. Of course, a starting point needs to be marked off. If you like, each contestant could have two chances.

Broom handles cut into short sticks can serve as batons. For the baton relay, have four to six contestants from each cabin. Make a line straight across for each cabin and then block it off evenly for the other three to five participants. Number 1 runs to number 2 with the baton, and number 2 takes it to number 3, etc. The cabin whose participants get to a set goal first is the winner.

If you want to have a fifty-yard or one-hundred-yard dash, these can be planned and the starting point and finish marked.

You can make awards for those who win first, second, and third place by using metal rim tags, the same as some camps use on the buddy board at the lake, and staple pieces of ribbon of three different colors to these. Write on them with magic markers, indicating the place and event. These can be given out in the dining hall the next day at breakfast. The cabin with the most points should be especially honored. You could make some kind of trophy for them.

Scavenger Hunt to Get Dessert

Plastic bags with enough candy bars for every camper in the cabin can be hidden for the cabins by staffers. Clues can be laid, beginning inside each cabin. For example, the campers in cabin 10 might go back to the cabin and find this first clue: "Go to the athletic hut on the athletic field for clue number 2."

When they find clue number 2, it reads, "Go to the steps of the Health Center for clue number 3." This would continue for five or six clues, the last one locating the bag of candy.

Hunt for Watermelons and Decorate Them

A watermelon can be hidden for every cabin. Each cabin is then given clues, similar to those used for hunting the bags of candy. After the melons are collected, someone can take them to the auditorium or some big place where they can be decorated. You could hunt the melons before supper and decorate them after supper, if you wish. Numbers should be put near the watermelon belonging to each cabin. Each cabin should then be given toothpicks, raisins, lemons, marshmallows, and the like to use in putting faces on the melons. The campers could bring hats or other things from their individual cabins to use in decorating their melon. A group of judges should choose first-, second-, and third-place winners. Winners could be given penny-candy rewards for their creativity.

Gold Rush

You can paint rocks gold, scatter them over the grounds, and let the campers hunt them. The cabin finding the most rocks, or rocks that make the biggest pile, could be declared the winner.

Staff Hunt

All staffers and guests could be assigned points that they are worth. These should be read out to the campers. The campers are then gathered where they cannot see and are led in a singspiration while the staffers and guests hide. When everyone has had time to hide, the bell is rung and campers begin hunting. After a reasonable length of time, the bell is rung to signal that the hunting is over. It is then time to reassemble. Every time a camper finds somebody, she takes that person to the person who led the singspiration. This leader records the staffer's cabin number and the worth of the points the person found. At the end, the cabin with the most points wins some candy.

Water Show

Campers in each cabin should elect people to compete in three swim areas and in the diving contest. The first area should be for nonswimmers, the second area for good swimmers, and the third area for those who have passed the greatest test of skill and endurance. Types of competition you might have in the first area (the area for nonswimmers) include

blowing a Ping-Pong ball from one point to the rope separating the areas. The person getting his ball to the rope without touching it is the winner.

Also, you might have first area contestants wear clothes over their bathing suits. When the whistle blows, they begin taking off clothes down to their bathing suit, run to the rope and back, and put back on the clothes. The person finishing first is the winner.

In the second area, divide the competitors into two groups. For example, if you have twelve cabins, put those in cabins 1-6 in one canoe and those in cabins 7-12 in another canoe. Have both canoes start from the same point. They must paddle with their hands on both sides of the canoes. The metal canoes are often light and fill with water but can be paddled even when full of water. The canoe reaching the rope first is the winner. All those in the winning canoe win points for their cabin.

In area 2, all competitors could secure a float and paddle these in a race to a certain destination.

In the third area, every competitor can be given a lighted candle. At a given signal they can swim a set distance. In order for someone to win, his candle must not go out. The winner is the person who gets to the set point first with his candle still lighted.

Sometimes a greased watermelon race is a good contest for third area campers. Just throw it in and give the signal, and whoever brings it ashore first is the winner.

In the third area, campers can compete in a diving contest with selected judges rating them on two dives each.

It is possible to have a canoe race by each competitor standing on the end of a canoe. Each bends his knees and moves up and down, making the canoe move forward toward a given point. If the lifeguards are good at rhythm swimming, the campers love it.

Creativity Contest

Each cabin could take camp life, activities, and personalities as the subject for some creative presentations. They could make up songs, perform a skit, or imitate camp personalities. These could be presented at a special program. If the cabin preferred, they could make a montage on camp (a collection of pictures and words glued to a large poster board). These should be built around camp life and could include special sayings, songs, events, goals. The montage should be explained to the audience.

A panel of judges could judge the creative presentations on:

(1) Creativity: 0-10 points

(2) Manner of Presentation: 0-10 points
(3) Good Development of Theme: 0-10 points
Each judge should total his points, and first-, second-, and third-place winners be announced.

If campers cannot make up original tunes, they can usually make up words about camp life that will fit familiar tunes. Then somebody who plays the guitar or piano can accompany the group as they sing. Sometimes a cabin might act out the nighttime pranks of the campers after the counselor has gone to bed, showing her exasperated efforts to control the group. Imitations of staff or program personalities are often delightful for campers.

Staffer TV Show

In my experiences with camping, the campers have always been responsive to takeoff shows imitating those who are popular in the entertainment world at the time. Sometimes this has taken the form of playing a record and pantomiming words and dance movements. Of course, a big part of making such a program go over has involved dressing as much like the entertainer would dress as possible. Staffers can collect jokes and weave them into a dialogue between people imitating Dolly Parton and Minnie Pearl, or others who are more popular at the time, such as Dudley Moore.

A soap opera, as the basis for a skit, can be hammed up. For example, our staffers made up a highly dramatic takeoff called "As the Stomach Turns." They chose some funny lines to fit into the drama.

One group of staffers used their instruments to create a band. They played clarinet, piano, banjo, and trombone on "Five Foot Two." They dressed like a 1920s band. One staffer came out with mustache, straw hat, and bow tie, and pantomimed "Five Foot Two" as if he was looking for his girl, as the band played. He began saying the words. On about the second run-through the back door opened. Down the aisle came a staffer about 5'2" dressed in a flapper-type dress with lots of makeup, throwing flower petals up the aisle, and sporting a rose between her teeth. The person who had been pantomiming met her, and they danced the Charleston to the hilarious response of the audience.

To plan a program of this type, consider the talents of the staff you have. What instruments do they play? Who can sing? Then talk about those personalities who are favorites with the teens of the day. Plan from there.

Human Checkers Game

Let the cabins select persons to be human checkers for this game. If you have twelve cabins, campers from cabins 1-6 can elect two checkers per cabin; and cabins 7-12 can do the same. They will be used in the game against each other. You need a large room where you can draw a checkerboard on the floor. Tie strips of black crepe paper as streamers around the campers selected from cabins 1-6 and red crepe paper streamers around those in cabins 7-12.

Choose two people to play the game. These could be two program personalities you think the campers would enjoy seeing play. Everybody needs to assemble around the checkerboard so they can see. Actually, people could see better if the board could be drawn on a raised platform in the middle of the floor. Spectators would arrange themselves in a circle around the platform. The two players should be given sticks with which to tap the human checkers when they want them to move. They also touch the square into which they want the checker to move. The checkerboard should be drawn like a real one and the game played by the same rules as regular checkers. More than one game could be going on simultaneously.

The checkers are first lined up on the board, all blacks on one side and reds on the other. When a checker is crowned, one person attaches himself to the back of the other. The game continues until someone wins.

Nature Hike

Everybody meets and lines up by cabin groups. Each group is given a list of nature items that they must collect and bring back from a hike, or things one person from the cabin can definitely say he saw. Examples include:
(1) An orange mushroom
(2) A catalpa leaf
(3) A mosquito hawk
(4) A frog
(5) A cardinal or quail (or other bird familiar to the area)
(6) A male pinecone
(7) A piece of fern
(8) Bush vetch (small purple wildflower)
(9) A common rockrose (yellow wildflower)
(10) A maypop
(11) A water lily or thistle
(12) Moss

The nature director needs to become familiar with the trees, wildflowers, mushrooms, insects, and birds that are common near the camp, and should arrange hikes earlier for those who choose to study nature. Those who have been on such hikes will be a special asset to their cabin groups. If you can afford a good set of field glasses, these will make bird watching much more fun.

At the close of the nature hike, the cabins assemble, and the counselors help check to see how many items have been found. The cabin with the most items wins. You could give some kind of prize or privilege to the winner.

A Barnyard Party

Ahead of time, every camper in each cabin should be assigned a different animal or bird. Each cabin, however, should be given the same assignment. Examples: cow, bear, goat, lamb, pig, rooster, pigeon, snake, frog, horse, dog, cat, or coyote. As they arrive at the party, everyone should begin making the sound of the animal assigned.

Section off groups with chairs and place a sign for each animal or bird on the wall where that group is to gather. When everybody has found his group, the members should work together to make a large brown paper bag look like the face and head of their animal.

Each group should have (1) a large brown bag, (2) scissors, (3) crayons, (4) construction paper, (5) glue, (6) pieces of ribbon or other odds and ends. Each group should elect a camper to model the bag. Of course, holes should be punched for the eyes. Have a fashion show, with judges chosen ahead of time. An announcer introduces the cabin number and the name of animal or bird, plus the name of the model. Each model then marches across the platform. You could use some music for background. The winners should be chosen on the basis of how much creativity the group displayed in making their bag look like the animal assigned them. Winners should be announced.

The staff could then do a hillbilly program. If somebody plays the banjo, the staff could lead the campers in singing songs such as "Old MacDonald Had a Farm." If anybody can clog dance, that would be good. You could have a regular barn dance.

TV Commercial Party

Ahead of time, the staff should assign TV commercials to each cabin. The cabin group should plan some kind of skit that will be a takeoff on the commercial. They are then judged when presented to the whole camp.

Nursery Rhyme Presentations

Each cabin should be assigned a different nursery rhyme such as "Mary Had a Little Lamb" or "Old King Cole." They could then make some kind of modern version, a funny takeoff, or another interpretation if they desire. The more costuming used, the better. These can also be judged.

The "Miss Camp Whatever" Contest (for Girls)

A "Miss Camp Whatever Contest" is always exciting to campers if it is well planned. Each cabin should choose a contestant. The person chosen should be somebody campers appreciate, who contributes to camp morale and displays character. But she also must have talent.

During rest periods, or whenever it fits the camp schedule, the music director and pianist (or whatever staffers are in charge) should meet with the contestants. They first need to hear the talent. If it is not appropriate or entertaining, time should be given in helping the person work up something that will be effective.

The girls will need practice in walking onto the stage, out on the ramp, etc. A couple of long, sturdy tables can be placed longwise, out from the front of the stage, to serve as a ramp. The contestants can walk out onto this as they are introduced. Those in charge of the contest should organize how they will introduce the program and they should plan to take turns with emceeing. They may need to set up some microphones and practice using these, if they are available. In introducing the contestants, something like the following could be included: (1) name, (2) hometown, (3) cabin number, (4) hobbies, (5) goals and dreams for the future, (6) any interesting facts about the family, such as number and ages of brothers and sisters, occupation of father, or influence of family on girl, (7) church and school activities and offices held in organizations.

The contestants and those in charge can decide what the girls will wear to be introduced and what they will wear for their talent presentations. After they have walked the ramp with musical background and been introduced, the talent can be presented. This should be arranged according to a variety in talent. For example, if possible, do not have two or three piano pieces played one after the other. At the close of the talent, the judges should announce three to six finalists. These will then answer an impromptu question.

The type of questions put into a hat should be decided on the basis of your type of camp, its programs, the persons attending, and their backgrounds. Ours was a Christian, missionary camp for girls. Here are some sample questions: (1) How did you become a

Christian? (2) What has your camp experience meant to you? (3) Who has influenced your life in a special way and how? (4) Either share some of your goals for the future, or share how you feel people can tell if you are a Christian.

Themes for the "Miss Camp Whatever Contest" could include an emphasis on some popular song the campers like. The song could be sung in the opening of the program. A backdrop could be painted if staffers are talented enough to handle this. You could decorate a stool or chair with ribbon, flowers, and the like, and place it in the center of the stage for the queen. Make a crown of gold paper and glue jewels on it, or buy a tiara-type crown to present. You could give the queen flowers and a book you think is appropriate. Decorations could include candles, greenery, spotlights, or the use of a slide projector for a spot. A stereo and appropriate records could be used in between, and as background music when needed (or a live music group or a pianist could play).

You could, of course, adapt this to a "Mr. Camp Whatever Contest" or turn it into a comedy by males dressing as females.

Prank Feature

Naturally, the playing of pranks is a part of camp life. I learned to encourage the staff to limit these. The features we used sometimes included pranks. I will describe some that went over well and how you can organize them.

1. Have two people hold a long string or rope at either end. One of the persons calls the names of several people to come up and put their teeth on the string. "I want to send a message across this string to my partner down there. Putting your teeth on the string will help conduct the message down to him," he says. After everyone is in place, he mouths something and says to his partner, "Did you get it?" The partner says he did not. They do the whole thing again and he asks, "Did you get it that time?" "No," he answers. "Well, let's try one more time. Now, keep your teeth on the string and concentrate. I said, 'How do you like my string of suckers?'"

2. Have someone say he wants to create a nature scene. He calls up people to be trees, rocks, a frog, a snake, flowers, the sun, and a mountain. Then he puts a sheet over the mountain and says, "This mountain is snowcapped." He grabs a hidden can of water. As he throws it over the head of the person playing the part of the mountain he says, "And every mountain has a waterfall."

3. Have two people compete in a needle-threading contest. They are seated in chairs side by side and handed a needle and a piece of thread. They are then told the contest should not be too easy, so two people will step forward to cover the right eye of each competitor. The secret is that the two covering the eyes have rubbed lipstick on their right hands. When they cover the right eyes of the competitors, they put lipstick on them. After the signal, the contestants thread their needles. One is declared a winner. They look at each other and get the joke.

4. Ask about five or six people to sit on the floor in a circle with their hands behind them. One person has been chosen ahead of time for a joke to be played on and a person to do it to him. The person chosen to do the prank sits beside the person to be done in and has lipstick on his hands. These two sit at the end of the circle farthest from the leader. The leader explains that whatever he does to the person sitting to his right, that person should repeat to the person to his right, and on down to the end of the circle. The leader begins "Itsy bitsy cheekie weekie," touching the cheek of the person on his right with the tips of the fingers of one hand. The next person says and does the same thing, on down the line, until the next-to-last person rubs lipstick on the cheek of the last person. The leader says "Other itsy bitsy cheekie weekie" as he rubs the other cheek of the person to his right. After this, the leader says "itsy bitsy fordy wardy" and rubs the forehead of the person to his right with the tips of his fingers. Next, the leader says, "itsy bitsy nosey wosey" and rubs the nose with the tips of his fingers. The leader closes with "itsy bitsy chinny winny" and rubs the chin of the person next to him. After all of these are passed down, the person at the end of the line is given a mirror to see the lipstick on his cheeks, forehead, nose, and chin.

5. This joke is called "There's a Bar Over Thar." The leader asks four to six people to line up beside him, standing side by side, with shoulders touching at all times. The leader says to the person beside him, "I will say 'there's a bar over thar,' and you say, 'whar?' Then I say, 'over thar,' and you point as I do." The leader begins, "There's a bar over thar." The second person in line asks "whar?" The leader answers "over thar," and points toward the right with the right hand. The second person says to the third person, "There's a bar over thar." The person asks "whar?" "Over thar" answers the second person, pointing with the right hand. This goes down the line.

At the end of the line, when the last person says,

"There's a bar over thar," number one answers. The leader begins again and says the same thing, except that he points with his left hand. Both hands are kept outstretched. After all of this goes down the line, the leader says the same thing, and as he says "over thar," he kneels, being sure everybody still stays close together. After everybody kneels, the leader begins the same way, "There's a bar over thar." When the second person asks, "whar?" the leader says "over thar." As he says this, he shoves into the next person, pushing the entire group over on the floor.

6. The person in charge explains that the staff has had a secret meeting and elected a Queen or King Staffer that they are prepared to honor. Two chairs are covered with a sheet. Between them is a gap under which sits a tub of water. (Putting a pillow in it is a safety precaution.) Two people are prepared to escort the person to her throne. The name of the king or queen is announced. He or she is escorted to the throne and told he or she will be crowned. The person in charge holds the crown ready and asks him or her to be seated for the crowning. He or she goes into the water and looks very shocked.

15
Encounter Programs

One emphasis of the church renewal movement has been in the area of encouraging deeper interpersonal relationships among church members. Much has been said about the superficiality of our contacts from week to week, that we put up a front of being on top when we are actually hurting inside, that we fear disclosing our feelings of love and admiration, as well as our feelings of anger and anxiety.

Teenagers are at a good point in their development for learning more authentic patterns of relating. They are questioning who they are, what they want out of life, what God is saying to them, and how they may build satisfying relationships. Encounter programs may contribute to such growth.

No person should feel forced to share anything he does not feel ready to share with a group. I remember attending a camping conference once where I felt highly threatened. We were divided into small groups of ten the first day and told we would participate in group activities for morning watch. The leader said, "You will become intimate with these ten people before the week is over. Each of you will know the other members of his group quite well before we leave." My response to being told with whom I would become intimate was to become closed and unresponsive.

If people have just met each other, sharing will be at a different level than with those who have known each other for years. Age and experience will have its effect, as well as personality types of members. Every group that interacts effectively must include some people who are open enough to spark participation. The leader must encourage respect between participants. Any persons you can invite who are trained counselors, psychologists, social workers, or pastors with training in pastoral care will be uniquely equipped to do encounter groups. However, let it be clearly stressed that the plans outlined in this chapter are not for use with in-depth sharing on the level of psychological problems.

Let me recommend the following books by John Powell as good sources for topics on encounter: *The Secret of Staying in Love, Fully Human, Fully Alive,* and *Why Am I Afraid to Tell You Who I Am?* All of these books have been published by Argus Communications, Niles, Illinois 60648; and many book stores carry them.

If you wish to emphasize communication, see *The Secret of Staying in Love* as a basis. An emphasis on emotions and the expression of these, as well as the levels of communication, can be found in *Why Am I Afraid to Tell You Who I Am?* In the book *Fully Human, Fully Alive* John Powell describes what makes a person fully alive and also explains how a person's vision of self, of others, and of the world affects his behavior. The survey he has developed includes: I. Who Am I? II. Who Are Other People? III. What Is Life? IV. What Is the Physical World? V. Who Is God?

A resource for group encounter using Transactional Analysis with special reference to the church is *Born to Love* by Muriel James. A group leader can increase his own insights through reading *The Becomers* by Keith Miller or *Glad to Be Me* by Dov Peretz Elkins.

The following encounter programs include some suggestions for music. However, it would be wise to check with the music director who leads youth and the young people themselves to discover their favorite religious music. Records by Keith Green have recently been popular, and some of these have very impressive lyrics for creating a worship mood for youth. (Example: Keith Green—"Song for the Shepherd"—by Birdsong Music.) Preferences and interests change, but the person planning the program needs to consider theme and appropriateness, as well as popularity.

Encounter Program 1
Emphasis: Sharing Personally and Praying in New Ways

Number people and arrange them into groups as they enter, no more than ten in any group. Play meditation music either from "Nature-Wilderness" (Thoreau-Werner) on the record by Warner Brothers called "Desiderata," or "I Cannot Hide from God" (Carmichael) on the record by Sacred-Stereo (Sacred Productions, Inc., Waco, Texas) called "The Restless Ones and Other Original Ralph Carmichael Songs." Have everyone concentrate on God's greatness, his power, and all that he has created. Then demonstrate a group doing a litany.

To make up a litany, every person in the group will make a circle and hold hands. One by one, each will make a sentence of thanks or praise to God for one specific thing. After each such statement, the entire group will say, "We praise thee, O God!" Then will follow a period of intercession in which every person in the group will ask God for something in one sentence. After each request, the entire group will say in unison, "We beseech thee, O God!" (See chap. 2 of this book.)

After this demonstration, the meditation music can be played again, and each group will simultaneously begin making up litanies (or the music and meditation may be omitted). Without delay, the group litanies can follow the demonstration. Then present "The Walls" (see chap. 12).

On posters around the walls or on a blackboard are written some areas of personal sharing. While music is played, people should remain in their groups, decide what they are willing to share, and then one by one share with each other in the group. Topics for sharing include:

(1) Share a time you were angry with someone; tell why; and tell how you coped with it.
(2) Share a time you felt particularly close to God; describe and explain why God seemed real.
(3) Relate a time when you were jealous of someone. How did you act? Of what were you jealous? How did you deal with your jealousy?
(4) Tell of some time when you feel your prayers were answered. Describe how they were answered.
(5) Describe the person, or persons, who have had the greatest influence on your spiritual growth and tell why.
(6) Share a time you felt inferior to someone else when this created a problem, and explain how you coped with the feelings.

Each group should now join hands and pray conversationally concerning the needs of those in the group. This means each person only prays one or two sentences at the time on a particular topic. Each person can pray as many times as he desires, or as there is time. When each group has prayed until ready to stop, the encounter program closes. You could then have refreshments and informal visiting.

(For a complete explanation of conversational prayer, buy the book *Prayer: Conversing with God*, by Rosalind Rinker, Zondervan Publishing House, Grand Rapids, Mich., 1959.)

Encounter Program 2
Emphasis: Dreams for the Future

For the first part of the program, groups of people will make montages (arrangements of pictures from magazines) on their dreams for the future. Arrange for groups with eight to ten people. Place numbers on the walls for the groups. Near these numbers place these items for each group:

(1) About ten to twenty magazines with lots of pictures
(2) Some newspapers that can be spread out and used for poster paper, or regular sheets of poster board
(3) Glue, masking tape, or clear tape
(4) Scissors (if not available, pictures can be torn out)

Everybody will look through the magazines for one or more pictures concerning their dreams for the future. These will be glued close together, all over the newspaper. Then each person will take turns showing and explaining the significance of the pictures he has chosen.

Have an informal talk by someone who is happy in what he is doing vocationally. Choose someone who will appeal to youth and who feels he is doing what God wants him to do. Have him tell how he came to feel this was God's place for him. Perhaps he could give experiences related to his vocation and tell how he feels he is serving God. Either before or after this talk, have someone to sing "His Gentle Look" by Ragan Courtney and Buryl Red, page 2 in *Sing 'N' Celebrate*!

The same groups could then get together again. Anybody in the group fairly sure of what he plans to do vocationally could role-play this for the group and let them guess. Then the group could give him feedback concerning whether they feel he has the personality, talent, and emotional makeup to do what he role-played. The kind of feedback given will vary according to how well people in the group know each other. Maybe it will be true with these young people, as with many others, that they try to seek God's leadership purely on the basis of emotions rather than facts and honest feedback. Such an activity as this could be valuable.

Divide into prayer partners of two or three people who will take their Bibles and go off to pray together concerning God's leadership in their lives. If it is pretty weather, and if it is possible, people could go outside and take walks. They could even have a walking prayer time. This would involve walking and talking conversationally with God instead of with each other.

Encounter Program 3
Emphasis: Adult-Teen Relationships

(Invite teenagers and their parents.)

Have the play "Conflict" or the play "Stable Bows and Living Arrows" presented (see chap. 13). Be sure the play is learned well and can be presented enthusiastically. Parts should be memorized. Before the play is presented, as people arrive, give them a number so they will know where to go for the discussion after the presentation of the play. Have numbers on the walls for the groups and have leaders already chosen and instructed. Put all adults together and all teens together. At the close of the discussions, have a panel of adults and teens, selected ahead of time, sit on the stage or where everybody can see. Have a leader who will begin and keep the ball going. Those on the panel should share things they learned about how teens and adults can better understand and cooperate with each other. A counselor or chaplain could then discuss communication.

Close with an informal singspiration. Have a guitarist, pianist, and song leader to conduct this. They should choose songs the adults sang when they were teenagers, as well as songs today's teens know and enjoy singing.

Serve refreshments and allow for informal visiting.

Encounter Program 4
Emphasis: An Informal Observance
of the Lord's Supper

Setting: In a central place, where everybody can see, erect a large, rough cross with spotlight on it. Also, it would be nice to have a large poster in the "One Way Poster Series" of the head of Christ, if it is available. This poster makes Christ look manly and is very large. Focus a spot or projector on the poster and cross.

Consider the total number of people expected and

arrange for groups with from six to twelve in each one. Put numbers around the walls where the groups should locate themselves. You could number people as they arrive or meet them and tell them to choose a group, establishing the maximum for each group.

As people arrive, have mood music playing. You could use "Behold the Lamb of God," "He Was Despised," "Surely He Hath Borne Our Griefs," "And with His Stripes," "All We Like Sheep," all from the *Messiah*, or you could play portions from the musical *Celebrate Life*, by Buryl Red and Ragan Courtney, published by Broadman Press, 1972.

Have ready ahead of time broken sections of brown loaves of bread to be placed on top of a box in the middle of each group. Also, place a large paper cup of grape juice on the box for each group.

As you begin, the leader will instruct everyone to focus his eyes on the picture of Jesus and the cross. He is to meditate on what Jesus did for him as the record is played of "Surely He Hath Borne Our Griefs" from the *Messiah*. The leader will explain the meaning of the Lord's Supper and how it was begun and will read Matthew 26:20-30. He will then take a piece of bread as a helper stands beside him and say, "Today, as we remember the broken body of Jesus, broken for our sins, I feed my neighbor and he feeds me. We are his body, fellow Christians who feed each other spiritually as we pray for each other amid suffering, sorrow, and testing. Will you now take the bread and feed your neighbor and let him feed you."

As this is done in all the groups, play the record of "In Remembrance of Me" from *Celebrate Life*. In fact, if you have a youth group who can sing this, they could do so at this time.

The music stops, and the leader takes the grape juice. "Now, as I give my brother to drink of the fruit of the vine, we remember the shed blood of the Lord Jesus that secured for us freedom from guilt. We are all of one blood, brothers in Christ, brought together by his love and sacrifice, united to God through the death of Christ. The old life has been destroyed. The new life of Christ has begun in us. You share the juice with your neighbor in remembrance of Jesus' death on the cross."

Continue to play "In Remembrance of Me" or something from the *Messiah*. The leader will then instruct the people in each group to bow their heads and join hands, as the "Hallelujah Chorus" from the *Messiah* is played.

Then everyone goes outside to a big bonfire already burning. It should have been stated, at least before the entire program started, that people would be given a chance to share their Christian testimonies at a bonfire. (Be sure the fire is set about forty-five minutes ahead of time.) When everybody is seated around the camp fire, the leader will say that anybody who wants to share any kind of experience where God has become real to him can do so informally, one by one.

Do not let this drag out, but allow enough time. Watch the audience and try to judge time properly. Close the period with a singspiration that has been arranged by someone who is a good director. Use a ukulele, if you can, or a guitar.

A meal should be prepared for the group as the last thing. Serve sandwiches, potato chips, drinks, and brownies or whatever suits the group. If this is used at an overnight event, you could allow the program to run until about 12 PM, sleep late the next morning, and serve a brunch about 11:30 AM.

Encounter Program 5
Emphasis: Acceptance of Self and of Others

As people enter, divide them into groups. Have numbers around the walls for the groups.

Begin with a talent presentation by youth from your church, those attending your camp, or whatever the setting. Invite people to do certain things, or have tryouts and select a variety of talent that is appropriate. Have a good master of ceremonies who will tell a few jokes, but not talk too much. Be sure he will speak out. Allow for about thirty minutes for the talent.

People are already arranged into groups, and each group should have a leader who already knows what to do. He should bring paper and pencils for everybody in his group. He instructs people to write down three things they like about themselves and three things they dislike. They need to be told these will then be shared with the group. There will be time allowed for feedback. Allow everybody to share the positive things first and go back and catch up the negative.

Ahead of time, have ten to twelve junior high or high school young people selected to be "in a fishbowl." Have ten to twelve college youth or young people in their early twenties to also share in this program. The fishbowl arrangement will involve having everyone sit on the floor in two groups: an inner circle and an outer circle—the inner circle being somewhat smaller than the outer circle.

To begin with, the junior high or high school youth make a circle and are inside the fishbowl. They are the only ones who can talk. The college students and young adults sit in a circle around the junior high and high school students. They are outside the fishbowl at first, and they simply listen. The audience also just listens.

The group inside the fishbowl will have been instructed ahead of time to discuss problems that they have with accepting others: what they dislike in others, characteristics that bug or annoy them, prejudices or fears about meeting and knowing people. They just talk to each other in a free, casual way, as though nobody else is present.

When the person in charge of the program feels that enough sharing has gone on, and before the audience gets too tired, he calls a halt to this part of the program. He also can encourage participants to stay on the subject, if necessary. He asks those inside the fishbowl to trade places with those outside the fishbowl. Now the older youth will react to what they heard and will share some insights and understandings they may have gained by now concerning the topic. The older youth may be able to reflect some insights and experiences that will aid the younger teens.

Close by having everyone pray in concert. This means everyone prays out loud at the same time. (See chap. 2 of this book.) A chaplain could then speak on "Accepting and Dedicating Myself."

Encounter Program 6
Emphasis: World Need and Christian Sharing

First, have a presentation by a young person who has grown up in another country as the son or daughter of missionaries, or someone who has served as a summer missionary, or a national who has become a Christian and is presently living in America. If it is more convenient, invite a furloughing missionary. The person might wear native dress, bring curios, and show slides. You could even use a person who has worked and witnessed among a neglected people in the United States, such as the migrants.

Before the person speaks, have a song leader direct the group in singing some familiar and appropriate missionary hymn. The person presiding over the program can lead in prayer and introduce the speaker. The speaker should be informal and allow for a question-answer session at the close of his presentation. He should discuss the work he did, the customs of the people, the needs of the people among whom he worked, and his personal experience with Christ.

After this presentation, have a short break for refreshments and visiting.

(If you cannot locate an appropriate speaker, or prefer, you could have the play presented, "If You Do It Unto the Least"—see chap. 13—as the first part of the program.)

Divide people into groups of not more than ten or twelve. Give each group a world map and appoint a leader. (World maps can be ordered free from the Foreign Mission Board, 3806 Monument Avenue, Richmond, Virginia 23230.) As a group, look at the map. In the light of current news, discuss problems and needs all over the world. Discuss: (1) What are we, or people we know, doing about needs of people around us or anywhere in the world? (2) What could we be doing? (3) Read John 4:34-38 and discuss.

Conclude each group with a period of prayer for missionaries, for people in need everywhere, and for compassion to care and to share.

Close the entire program with a good presentation of the choral reading "Jesus Shall Reign," included in chapter 12. The reading should be memorized.

16
Use of Devotional Thoughts

The success of every aspect of camp relates directly to the depth of preparation. Some devotional thoughts are directed at staffers, some at teenagers, and some at children. The purpose of this section is to inspire you to study and plan for meaningful devotional experiences with all who attend camp.

Many staffers could sometimes be inspired by fresh devotional thoughts. The director will know intimately his own staff and camp. I do not presume to believe you will take the devotionals I have written and learn them as they are. However, I have touched on topics I found appropriate through my sixteen years of experience. I trust there is adequate information in each of these to spur your own study and thinking. I ultimately came to give one devotional talk to my staffers per week at regular staff meetings.

The devotional thoughts for teenagers and children might help you with ideas if you prepare any devotional materials for campers. I wrote a devotional booklet for teenagers each summer which was given to each camper at our seven-day camp. Two or three partners met every morning and used the devotional booklet as the basis for their time together. They also carried their Bibles and concluded the period with prayer. I usually gave individual sheets of devotional thoughts to children to share with prayer partners a couple of times a week during the shorter camps.

You might need to speak at vespers or in cabin devotionals and be able to use the material in some of my devotionals as a springboard for your thoughts. Or some of your staffers may need some help in preparing devotionals and could be pointed to this material.

Staffer Devotional 1
Open Your Life Godward

Read James 4:7-12.
James reminded us that opening our lives to God can make a difference. There will be power to overcome evil. We will be made aware of our sins and confess them. If we draw close to God, he will draw close to us.

If staffers are to renew their strength, they need a daily time away from the camper to become relaxed and receptive. The preacher and author Dr. John A. Redhead says that tension is what shortcircuits the power God can give. We need time to be quiet and release every muscle. We can focus our minds on truths of his Word that assure us of his power, his place, his goodness.

Lewis Sherrill says that for some people life is a treadmill, for some a saga, and for others a pilgrimage. In days past there was used a wide wheel, and a prisoner was used to tread around this wheel all day. This helped work the mill. This is a treadmill existence. It goes nowhere. It is boring and monotonous. It has a deadening quality about it.

No matter how purposeful your work at camp may be in the beginning, it can easily become mere routine. Constantly seek to discover fresh approaches to your work. Getting to know new people can help. Cultivating a friend on a deeper level can add new zest. Learning a new skill can be challenging. Opening your life daily to let God's Spirit renew can revitalize your work.

A saga is a medieval story in which there is a hero or family to be followed in many adventures. The saga teaches men to see and honor the humanness of the natural virtues, such as courage, patience, endurance, and self-sacrifice. The saga made life entirely humanistic. In this technological age, many see no need for resources and goals above the human and physical. Today scientists are doing many of the things once ascribed to God. The church steeple used to be the tallest structure in a town and appropriately symbolized the superior place of God and religion. But today many high-rise apartments, factories, and commercial buildings rise above the church. This correctly pictures the place many modern men give to human power and self-elevation. As a college student said some years ago, "We have everything we need. I see no need for God."

The true Christian pilgrim sees the eternal amid the physical. He knows real life is rooted in God and will last forever. He has his eyes set on a city not built with human hands but eternal in the heavens. He is on a pilgrimage which overcomes the treadmill and rises above the saga. He is never alone. He can put his hand into the hand of God and be guided by a person wiser than he is.

When Andrew became a Christian, he began to work in a chocolate factory in Holland. To the other workers, it was just a way to make a living. To Andrew it was a mission field, and he was a Christian witness under orders. Foul language became used less often, and the woman with the vilest mouth of all was profoundly changed by the influence of Andrew.

Later God led Andrew to be his witness throughout the Communist-dominated countries of Europe. He found little bands of faithful Christians who needed his help and encouragement. His pilgrimage included a call. It involved a companionship between him and Christ. Life was rich and purposeful.

As we open our lives to God each day, we can rise above our fears. Dr. Paul Tournier, a famous Swiss psychiatrist, says all people are gripped by fear. He says some people feel they are inferior because of their fear, but everyone has fear.

Many of the tasks you face at camp may be fearful at first. You may find that relating to many different kinds of people creates an anxiety within you. The thing to do is to admit your fears to yourself and to ask God to help you refuse to be controlled by them. Do not put yourself down for having fear. Let it push you to grow.

Fear gripped Jeremiah when God told him to go and speak in his name. Jeremiah said he was young and could not speak, but God replied, "All to whom I send you . . . you shall speak" (Jer. 1:7, RSV).

God said to Joshua: "As I was with Moses, so I will be with you; I will not fail you or forsake you. Be strong and of good courage; . . . Only be strong and very courageous, being careful to do according to all the law which Moses my servant commanded you; turn not from it to the right hand or to the left, that you may have good success wherever you go. . . . Be strong and of good courage; be not frightened, neither be dismayed; for the Lord your God is with you wherever you go" (Josh. 1:5-7,9, RSV).

Staffer Devotional 2:
Jesus, Master Communicator

This is a day of mass communication. Television has brought the sights and sounds of the world crashing into our minds, our senses, and our consciences. We see starving children in Cambodia right in our homes. Political leaders from all over the world tell us their views. Violent conflicts are vividly portrayed.

Commercials tell us what to buy. Every product is glorified as the best. We are told how to belong to the Pepsi Generation and how to have sex appeal, the cleanest wash, and the youngest skin.

Salesmen knock on our doors. On the streets we are met with billboards and handouts. The daily paper is brought to our mailboxes. On the way to work, the radio blares out the latest music.

We are bombarded by every means of communication. Such a flood of contact has created a skeptical generation. We question every message. After all, we have been cheated. Many products do not do what they promise to do. The world is full of fakes. We have been manipulated and hurt many times by people who failed us.

How can Jesus make himself known to this present world? He wants to use us. If we study the ways he communicated the truth as revealed in the New Testament, we will find some helpful guidelines. We will discover ways we can help make Christ known to a world that needs him today, just as he was needed two thousand years ago.

In John 1:14-18 we are told that God made himself known to us by becoming a person like us. If we listen to birds chatter in the trees, we know they communicate. Do we know what they are saying? No, because we are not birds. To make himself clearly known to us, God had to allow himself to be limited by the flesh, emotions, and voice of humans.

John the Baptist made announcements to public crowds that Jesus was coming and was so great that John was not fit to untie Jesus' sandals. When Jesus arrived, John saw him and said, "There he is. He is the lamb who will die for all men. We will find forgiveness through him."

Jesus taught men the truth by becoming personally involved with them. This meant he became vulnerable. When he went to the garden of Gethsemane to ask God not to make him go to the cross, he took James, John, and Peter. They were his closest friends.

He was in agony over the thought of dying the painful death of a common criminal. "Please pray with me!" he told them.

They waited while he went off alone to pray. He was in great emotional pain. He wanted to be obedient to God, but he feared the cross. His friends did not carry his burden and bear him up. They went to sleep instead. What a disappointment!

There are times when we all need others to pray on our behalf. Sometimes we are physically ill. We may be depressed and find we simply cannot pray and believe. We need our Christian friends to believe and lift us up to God. But involvement with people means we will sometimes be disappointed.

Jesus found that James and John had the wrong idea about being great. They argued over who should sit on Jesus' right and left when he came into his kingdom. They knew he would some day be all-powerful. They wanted to have position and authority above other men. They had walked the country roads with Jesus. They had seen him perform miracles of mercy. They had loved and felt close to him, but they did not understand that his mission was one of service. He tried still to teach them that they sought rewards that would not enrich their lives as dying to self would do.

Peter was upset and scared when Jesus was taken prisoner. He followed from a distance. Surely he felt that the bottom had dropped out of his life. The star of hope that led him into meaningful service had just been snatched out of the sky of his life. He was wandering in the darkness of despair. The companion who had walked with him and led him to fish for men now left him lonely. When people began to accuse him of being a follower of Jesus, Peter said he did not even know Jesus. After denying Jesus three times, Peter went off to cry. The pain he felt was deep, and it spread throughout his body. He hated himself and felt he had lost his way.

How did Jesus communicate with these closest friends who failed him? He was understanding, accepting, and forgiving. On finding that the disciples simply could not keep their eyes open, Jesus said, "Well, go ahead and sleep." He understood their weakness. Maybe they were emotionally exhausted by all the shocking events that ultimately led to Jesus' death.

Jesus continued patiently to teach James and John that their idea of power and position was not the key to real life.

Peter experienced forgiveness and acceptance. I think it came after Jesus died and rose again. Peter had gone fishing with a group of the disciples. They had fished all night and caught nothing. Jesus appeared and told them to throw the net on the right side of the boat. They caught a net so full that it broke.

After the fish was cooked, Jesus began serving the disciples. Jesus approached Peter and asked him three times if he loved him. Peter became more anxious each time and more adamant in his reply. "Yes, Lord," said Peter, "You know that I love you." Jesus replied, "Feed my lambs. . . . Tend my sheep. . . . Feed my sheep" (John 21:15-19, RSV).

Jesus was continuing to communicate that Peter was accepted, that he should go back to the job Jesus had called him to do—to love and serve persons with a spirit of caring Jesus had shown him. Peter was not cast out because he was dishonest and unfaithful; he was still accepted.

Sometimes we are so disappointed in our own weaknesses that we begin to feel we do not belong to Christ after all. But I believe Jesus would say to us as he said to Peter, "I've forgiven you. You must forgive yourself. You must not wallow in self-pity and remorse. You must get on with caring for others and letting me love them through you."

The truth of the gospel is that God accepts our brokenness. God calls us to communicate this same acceptance to others.

I think of a teenager who is seventeen. We will call him John. He wakes up thinking about alcohol. He thinks of pizza with beer. He was confronted by two teenage friends who told him of things he did that he did not remember. They said these happened after many alcoholic drinks. I am his counselor. He began keeping a record of all he drinks. We put it on a calendar. "I did not realize I drank something every day," he said. But there it was on the calendar—he drank something alcoholic every day.

John is in a stage of acceptance and denial about his drinking. He admits he badly needs help one day, and the next day is not sure he has a problem.

I confront him with the truth and then seek to support and love him. How difficult it is to do this in the right spirit. I must love and accept him but help him see alcohol as his enemy. I have wanted to pray with him. As we talked about religion, he told me about his Unitarian faith. He does not attend worship, nor does he know God in Christ. I believe God, through Christ, can love him enough to help him get the victory. How I can be the instrument for such healing is a challenge.

One afternoon I realized that my being critical of

his drinking was coming across to him as rejection of him. I changed moods by saying, "But I really do love you." I began telling some funny stories. He told a delightful joke I began telling other staff members. He followed me as I shared it and as I told people it was John's joke. I hugged him and left for the day. It will be a long, daily struggle for John to overcome alcohol. He needs God's instruments to help him.

I have become friends with a lovely member of my church who is battling cancer. We visited one Sunday afternoon. She shared interesting aspects of her life I had not known. I asked if she would like for us to pray together. "Oh yes!" she said.

We listed our concerns and prayed for each one after they were listed. God was present with us, communicating himself in listening and caring.

To communicate the truth about God, we must care for others. We must become involved with them. We must become vulnerable to hurt and misunderstanding. We must accept our failure and keep opening our lives to God's grace and his purposes.

Staffer Devotional 3:
The Conflict Within

Read Romans 7:15-25.

In this passage Paul referred to the struggle inside himself between good and evil. He said he knew what was right but lacked the power to do the right. Surely we can all identify with this helpless feeling.

Have you ever had the need to lose weight? The very day you set down your resolution to go on a diet you probably felt hungrier than normal. Maybe you even were invited to eat out with friends you especially wanted to enjoy.

I can remember making such a resolution about weight and praying about it throughout the day. This treatment focused my mind on the problem and made it worse. I ultimately learned that the more I did to be involved in other things, the less time I had to concentrate on food. Focusing the mind on everything but food and staying busy was important.

I have had a need to break habits that bound me. I could ask God to help, but I must structure my time consciously so I would not be tempted. I must be with other people, go to other places, get out of the usual routine in order to change these habits. We often allow ourselves to be tempted by placing ourselves where others are doing things we want to stop doing.

Many times young people tell me that they have smoked pot for a couple of years. They see that it is hindering them from achieving what they would like

to achieve, but they still go out with their friends who get "high." They know they will not participate. I have never seen such action work out well. The young person almost invariably falls back into doing what his crowd does.

When we consider the struggle inside, we can look at David in the Old Testament. He was called "the man after God's own heart." One summer evening David walked out onto the roof of his house and saw a beautiful woman, Bathsheba, bathing. Rather than turning his attention elsewhere, he allowed his lustful eyes to enjoy the sensual beauty of this woman until sin overcame him. He sent for her. She was brought to him and slept with him. She became pregnant; and then he was faced with what to do about her husband, Uriah (2 Sam. 11).

David's men brought him information indicating that Uriah, a soldier, was stationed at a particular battle site. David had his military leaders arrange to send Uriah up front in battle where he would be killed.

Nathan, the prophet, confronted David with his sin (2 Sam. 12:1-14) and David repented. (Read Ps. 51 to know exactly what David said as he confessed.) Interestingly enough, Nathan was the accuser who meted out God's judgment, but God's word of forgiveness was also spoken to David by Nathan.

Nathan then told David that there would be consequences of his sin. When we confess our sin, God does forgive us. However, there are results of that sin that cannot be changed. For example, disruptions in David's family relationships could not be prevented. Uriah could not be brought back to life. Much of the evil in the world is a result of the poor choices and evil actions of men. We all suffer from these. Whether we lose a loved one killed in a wreck by a drinking driver or have respiratory problems because of air that is polluted by nicotine and nuclear wastes, we all share some common suffering.

In my own life my poorest decisions have been made on the basis of my feelings. As psychiatrist Eric Berne tells us, our feelings center in the Child personality inside us. We all have three personality states: Parent, Adult, and Child. The Parent personality tells us wrong from right and is made up of how we have been taught to behave by those who have raised us, our teachers, and preachers. Our Adult personality is the one that looks at facts. In the Adult we raise logical questions such as, "If I do this, what will be the results?" Making decisions out of our Child personality is like turning our life over to a five-year-old. We lack judgment.

David looked at Bathsheba and allowed his Child personality to do what he felt like doing. Had he consulted his Parent personality, the moral teaching he had received would have told him that what he wanted to do was wrong. Had he consulted his Adult personality, he might have said, "If I do as I wish, where will that lead? How will that affect my family? Even though being with Bathsheba now may be delightful, will I be happy with the results of this action later?" As Christians, we need to grow strong Adult personalities in order to build satisfying lives.

Read James 1:12-16.

Staffer Devotional 4:
Seeking Our Place

Read Luke 15:11-32.

We are all seeking a sense of place and of belonging. One way of looking at this parable is to see it as two sons seeking their places. Parables were often used by Jesus. *Harper's Bible Dictionary* defines a parable as "a short fictitious narrative based on a familiar experience and having an application to the spiritual life."

In studying family relationships, psychologists have discovered that the interactions affect what roles various members of the family play. For example, Adlerian psychology says that often the eldest child tries hard to please his parents by being ambitious and hard working. More persons who have graduated at the head of their classes were firstborn children than not.

When the firstborn child is very industrious, it is common for the secondborn to refuse to compete with the firstborn. He may become the "bad" child if his brother is the "good" child. He may turn to sports if the firstborn makes excellent grades in school.

In this story of the prodigal son, Jesus tells about two brothers. The eldest is hard working and always seeks to please his father. The youngest sounds like the second child who takes the role of the "bad" child. He will not compete with his "too good" brother. He wants the inheritance his father would normally give him at his death. The father does not seem to warn and fuss with him. He seems simply to give in and give him the money.

The young son goes far away to party. He has many friends as long as he has money. But when the money is gone, he is alone. In our day we can picture such a boy having pot parties and beer busts. He probably would have a sporty car and drive fast. He would probably be with many girls.

We are told that this youngest son went to work feeding the pigs when his money was gone. He was a Jew. To Jews, pigs were unclean. They did not eat pork, and tending such animals was probably an indication of truly being at the bottom of the barrel. He even became so hungry that he longed to eat the food he fed the pigs.

In his degraded state, this young man had a flash of insight. He realized that even his father's servants had plenty to eat. He decided to humble himself before his father and offer to become a hired servant. He would confess that he had sinned against heaven and his father, and he would admit that he was more deserving of being a servant than a son.

We are told that his father saw him from a distance and ran to meet him. Leslie Weatherhead, world-famous preacher and author, points out that for an Eastern gentleman to run was undignified and was not often done in public. Therefore, such action shows the abandon that was rooted in pain and caring.

The party that was held to celebrate was a way of rejoicing. Putting the robe, shoes, and ring on the son all affirmed the father's forgiveness. The relationship was restored. Weatherhead points out that the sin of the past may mean it will take time and patience to restore the son to health and clear thinking. Sin can be forgiven, but its results may be difficult or impossible totally to overcome.

This makes me think of one of my students who was hooked on cocaine. Her mother took her home, where the pain of withdrawal caused her to scream and cry. She is finding it slow business to totally overcome drugs. She has not yet completed her high school work, although she is nineteen. She passed a nursing technician course and hopes later to complete high school and other training.

In this story of the prodigal son, the father did not preach to the son, but accepted him lovingly. He realized that the trip into a far country of sin and lostness had meted out enough pain. The son had learned and now needed love and understanding. In inviting the neighbors, he showed no shame over his son, only joy.

But what of the "good" son? He was accepted. All the father had was available to him, but he could not feel accepted. He had high standards and looked down on his wayward brother. This firstborn son believed that he should be rewarded and that his brother should be punished.

Perhaps he was too hard on himself and this caused him to be harsh and condemning with his brother. It seems that he was a perfectionist, was driven. His father's love and acceptance seems never to have been deeply felt and believed by him. It is sad to see a young person strive all his life for his father's approval and never get it. But how much sadder to have his father's acceptance and not experience and enjoy it.

The elder son was not able to rejoice over the return of his brother. Therefore, anger was creating an atmosphere of isolation within the heart of this sad young man.

Jesus was never harsh with those who were beaten down by their sin. But he was harsh with those who were self-righteous, like the Pharisees. The elder brother in this story sounds like a sour Pharisee. The love of his father was as available to him as it was to the prodigal. He simply was not in touch with his own need. He needed love and forgiveness, but his pride walled him away from his father's love forever.

Where the parents in a home compete with each other, much conflict is set up. This creates a home environment in which competition between siblings is much more common than in homes where parents trust and cooperate.

At camp we need to create an atmosphere of acceptance. Staffers need to be committed to *cooperation* as they work with each other, not *competition*. If staff members begin to see who can be the *best* at everything, this can create a desire to see who can be the most *popular*. We do not need a contest between staffers. We need the sense that each person has a place to fill, and we are pulling together. We are all seeking to let God be the leader and to lift him up. A variety of personalities among staffers is important. We need some who are more talkative than others and some who are quieter. We need some who are musical and some who are athletic. Let us work together like an orchestra. Let us harmonize to make music to honor Christ, our conductor.

Read Romans 12:3-8.

Teenage Devotional 1: Our Sins Find Us Out

Read Psalm 37:1-7.

It is true that people who are dishonest sometimes get rich. Men who sleep with other women besides their wives may seem to get away with such behavior for years. The home may seem to be satisfying and the man might enjoy a fine reputation in the community, but there will be a day of judgment.

Judgment may already be at work in the inner life of the one who has sinned. Leslie Weatherhead tells of a woman who began sleepwalking and carried all her precious jewelry away from the house and discarded it. The jewelry had been given to her by her husband who was away in service.

She came to Dr. Weatherhead asking him why she would do such a thing. After they had worked together for sometime, it came out that she had been unfaithful to her husband. She had hidden her sin. Other people did not know. But her unconscious mind was telling her she did not deserve the jewelry her husband had given her. She faced her sin and asked God to forgive her. She reaffirmed her marriage vows.

A young man I know has been on drugs as long as I have known him. His medication for seizures began doing no good because he was also drinking alcoholic beverages. Tom, we will call this young man, said he would give up alcohol but loved other drugs too much.

Tom attended our school longer than most of our students but never finished. He has normal intelligence and a good personality. His future, however, does not look bright.

Tom talked to me about his father making lots of money. On occasion, Tom told of underhanded ways his father cheated to have more money. This seemed to impress Tom.

Certain disruptions in the family unity began being attributed to Tom's father. Tom felt his father should see a counselor and asked me how he could get his father to go for help. I told Tom he could do nothing more than encourage his father.

I suggested to Tom that the only person he has any real control over is himself. I told Tom his father has lived above the laws of God and of mankind and that such behavior is catching up with him and spilling over onto the family. I told Tom some of his behavior seems to be a copy of his father. I said, "I see you trying to live above the laws of God and mankind."

Tom did not want to accept this. I pointed out his laziness, his illegal use of drugs. He is not following the laws of God and mankind. He said, "Now wait a minute, Miss Sanders. I do work on weekends you don't know about. And it isn't illegal, either."

"Tell me about it," I said.

"Well, I don't actually sell drugs. People call and let me know they want them. I call the pusher, and that's what I get paid for, the contact."

I kept confronting Tom with his twisted way of thinking. He could not be more guilty if he put the drugs into the hands of those who call him. I told him that the laws of God will break him.

I believe God's moral laws are as established as his

physical laws. If you drop a brick out of a window on the tenth floor of a building, it will drop to the ground because of the law of gravity. The brick will never fly upward, no matter how many times it is dropped. This law of gravity is established.

God's laws are laid out for us in the Ten Commandments. Read Exodus 20. When we do not honor God as first, our lives get unbalanced. If we neglect regular worship, we begin to get confused in our values and do not know where to turn in our time of need. If we do not grow to the point where we can appreciate our parents and value good things they have done for us, our sense of who we are can become more confused. We need a feeling of belonging to a family, a sense of connectedness. As we mature, we discover there comes a time when we should give to our parents, not merely expect them to give to us.

Stealing can easily become a way of life, especially when people get away with such behavior. I once had a student tell me that he stole all kinds of tools. He said he started frequenting places where construction was going on and where people left tools lying around. He kept getting by with such behavior. I tried to help him see that one day such behavior would catch up with him. What a different feeling we have when we do honest work for what we earn. There is a sense of pride and well-being.

I do believe that what we sow by thought and action certainly affects what we reap later. It behooves us to guard what we read and focus our minds on when we realize that what goes into our minds ultimately comes out in action.

As Dr. John A. Redhead, Presbyterian minister and author, has said, the mind is like a barrel. We pack all sorts of influences into it. Later, they become the springboard for our actions.

Teenage Devotional 2: A Rebellious Life Can Be Productive

Much is said about the rebellion of youth, their fight against "the Establishment." Rebellion has a natural place in the lives of youth. Jesus was a rebel. He rejected the established religious life and ritual of his day. He taught that true religion was a matter of the heart, not of dead forms and rituals. He said religion should be expressed in actions of justice and mercy. He said giving tithes and once-a-year alms or confession were not adequate.

Martin Luther was a rebel in his day. He had such convictions about the truth of God that he stood against an entire church. It was the faith of one man against the accumulated beliefs of Bible scholars and church clergy that had built up over a period of many years. How presumptuous and proud could a young monk be?

I am sure it has become a fact of history that its young people saved Indonesia from a Communist takeover some years ago. They did not merely talk. They acted. Of course, the young have had much to do with the movement of human rights in our own country in this generation.

But how often do young and old burn out their energies in merely criticizing? Too often practical suggestions and support of the positive are entirely missing. Sometimes young people allow themselves to be carried away by the emotion of the moment. This has often led to support of godless, hate-filled movements.

The church has been under severe attack by the young in this generation. But how are they helping the church? Can they do it by pulling out in disillusionment and spending their time on the secular?

Those who say the church is full of hypocrites need to stick with it. Through their genuineness, they can strengthen true Christianity. Those who say the church is self-centered and will engage in no social action may very well be the ones to lead it into such action.

Sure, this would take time, patience, and prayer. But these are the very keys to the development of Christian character. Were not these the essential tools Jesus and Paul used in helping people grow into the Christian life?

Jesus was perfect and still hung in there with disciples who fought over positions of prominence. Is not something wrong with mere Christians who cannot take the church's weaknesses? How can we be too good for it if Jesus was not?

Young people have a touch with their present age that those who are older naturally lack. Those who are more mature have learned some valuable things through their many experiences. What is needed to make the church vital in our day is an openness between the "now" and the "other" generations. Each has something to share.

Without the young, the church indeed gets into the worst sort of rut. More adults need to realize they do not know all the answers; nor are they always right. The young need also to be willing to listen and not assume they know it all. Programs and activities of the church need shared ideas and leadership of the now and the other generations. Such involves resiliency and openness.

The modern missionary movement was ushered in by a group of young seminary students who formed a prayer group. Can we count on any of our Christian youth to form prayer groups that new vitality may grip the Christian churches of America? Our nation can rise and overcome indifference with the prayers and support of its young for the cause of truth and justice.

Read Psalm 145:1-7; Ecclesiastes 12:1; Isaiah 40:28-31.

Teenage Devotional 3: Put the Kingdom of God First

Read Luke 12:14-31.

Jesus had much to say about the kingdom of God when he was here on earth. In his passage in Luke, Jesus described the farmer who is caught up in amassing wealth. His crops have become so productive that he has used every barn and still has run out of storage space. He ponders the problem before retiring for the night and decides he will begin the next day to build bigger barns. He rejoices that now he can relax and party. *The Living Bible* refers to his plans to enjoy wine, women, and song.

That night the farmer dies, and Jesus, who was telling the story to a crowd, raised the question of who will get this wealth the farmer has spent his life producing. Jesus even called him a fool.

What is the kingdom of God (or the kingdom of heaven)? Such a kingdom involves the reign of Christ in the human heart. This begins with a confession of our own lostness and need. We receive God's forgiveness and turn our lives over to him. The direction of our life is changed. What was first in our thoughts and desires has been replaced. We have given Christ the reign of our lives and are going to seek daily to follow him.

As a thirteen-year-old girl, I sat listening to my minister, Dr. Shands. I felt such a sense of guilt that I went down the aisle to confess openly. Dr. Shands suggested that I begin asking God every day what he wanted me to do. I did this and began to see that I had a life to offer in more useful ways than I had realized.

My twin sister and I walked to town and church by way of Alabama Street. I began to notice some elderly people on this street who seemed lonely. There was a couple who sat on the porch that I began stopping to visit. A man who had a nervous condition was bothered with a jerking neck. We often talked. I heard that workers were needed to help with a Bible school among some black children. I volunteered to help.

During my first year at the seminary, we were urged to engage in some kind of volunteer ministry. I chose Corsair Crippled Children's Hospital. That first visit was painful. Children on crutches or in wheelchairs and babies in casts from toe to thigh brought tears I was fighting hard to hide. I thought, *This is not the place for me. It is too upsetting.* But I went back and learned to love and enjoy these precious children. My pity changed to admiration. They loved our Sunday School with its stories and motion songs.

Realizing I had something to give and asking God to help me when I felt afraid and inadequate were new experiences for me. There was some indication that the kingdom of God was beginning to rule my life. I wish I could say the work of this kingdom of God was always evident, but I cannot.

What do we put first in our lives? Can people see that the kingdom of God has set up a work of love in and through us?

Are we so caught up in being popular that God has no chance to guide us? He will let us rush into all sorts of foolish decisions; but if we keep our eyes fixed on ideals of his kingdom, we will live purer and healthier lives.

A young girl with whom I was counseling told me about a friend of hers who had had an abortion several years before. Said my friend, "Everytime she babysits and holds a child on her lap, the tears begin streaming down her face."

I have never talked to a young woman who was pregnant out of wedlock who was not disturbed. One such young woman fluctuated from day to day about whether to keep the baby or put it up for adoption. She knew she was not prepared to make a good living and care properly for the baby, but amid her struggle she said, "But in carrying this baby, I already love it."

Life is so arranged that God's moral laws make life more orderly and manageable. Harnessing the sexual urge and letting God guide in its expression will lead to deeper, more lasting satisfactions. If God is not first, pressure to be accepted by the crowd can lead to an expression of sexual feelings beyond what a young person can handle.

If the kingdom of God is first in our lives, this will not mean we will not have any interest in material things. Our life in this world is dependent upon the material. Poverty does not honor God more than wealth. The person who makes more money has more to give to missions. But the question is whether material things are our first concern. The farmer in the story Jesus told had the wrong attitude toward wealth. He spent his life earning it for his selfish pleasure only.

Jesus reminded us that investment in the kingdom of God means we should worry less than others because storing our treasures of thought, ministry, and wealth in the vault of his kingdom will produce the highest dividends. Such an investment involves no risk of loss. The dividends of such investing will pay off forever and ever.

Devotional for Children 1:
Loving Myself and My Brother

Read 1 John 3:1-2,11-18.

The Bible also tells us: "But you shall love your neighbor as yourself" (Lev. 19:18, RSV). This verse makes it clear that we are to love ourselves, as well as our brother. If I hate myself, I cannot love others. If I don't accept myself, with my strong points and my weak ones, I will be critical of others.

The person who makes fun of others is uncomfortable with himself. A friend of mine became upset with Bob in the first-grade class she teaches. There was a pupil named James who did not have as much ability to think and learn as most of the pupils. Bob always tried to sit close to James at lunch to trick him out of some of his food. Once Bob promised James he would buy him a candy bar at recess if he would give him his piece of chicken. James agreed, and Bob ate the chicken. At recess the teacher saw James standing by while Bob ate a candy bar and teased, "You can't have any candy! You can't have any candy!

Do you make fun of people who are not as smart as you are in school? Who gave you the mind you have? You did not have anything to do with the kind of powers to think that were given you when you were born.

A mother who is expecting a baby may be poor and not able to afford the right kind of food and care from a doctor. This can cause her baby to be born with less thinking and learning ability.

Thank God for the mind you have. Develop a sense of respect for all people, regardless of how quickly or how slowly they learn.

Do you ever call people of other races by nicknames? The Bible tells us that God loves all races. See Acts 10. Peter learned this truth from his experience: "And Peter opened his mouth and said: 'Truly I perceive that God shows no partiality, but in every nation any one who fears him and does what is right is acceptable to him'" (Acts 10:34-35, RSV).

Some of the people who came to the United States from England in the early days of our history built large plantations. Slave traders were going to Africa and chaining the people as slaves and bringing them to work on these plantations. Our ancestors began to think of blacks as less valuable than whites. This has been changing a lot in recent years, but sometimes people are still unable to love themselves. This causes uncomfortable feelings inside. So some people still choose blacks or Spanish-speaking people or Indians to look down on so they feel better for a while.

This is wrong. Jesus taught us to love all people. An important question you might ask yourself is: Who made me white? God could just as easily have made us black. If any of us who are white suddenly changed to black, but had the same mind, body, and talents, would we then become worth less? Of course not!

I was once conducting a discussion group of teenagers. In this group was a young man who had great problems in talking so that we could understand him because he had cerebral palsy. This is a disease that twists the body and cripples people. People with this disease walk with great difficulty and have problems even trying to pick up things.

Every time this boy tried to talk, others in the group laughed. I was angry. I had a serious talk with them about their ugly behavior. Oh, that we could have loving feelings for all people! Only God can give us these.

If we are Christians, we should think how Jesus lived. He met a man who was blind and healed him. He told a man who could not walk to take up his bed and walk. The man discovered he was healed.

We may not heal people as Jesus did, but we can love and accept them. We can treat them the same way we would like to be treated. If we experience God's love, that should help us accept ourselves better. Feeling his love for us should help us love and accept all persons.

Devotional for Children 2:
Jobs Made More Important

Read Matthew 4:17-25.

Fishing was a fine job to have in Jesus' day. There were great seas and lakes in which to fish in Israel. Fishing was hard work and took patience. It was honest work, done in all kinds of weather.

These men whom Jesus called to leave their fishing jobs were needed as his followers. He wanted men to travel with him whom he could teach about the truth of God, so they could teach others. He knew his work would soon be over. He trained these fishermen, and others, to carry on a ministry of healing, teaching, praying, driving out evil spirits, and taking care of the needs of many people.

When God calls, he does not always tell us to become missionaries or preachers. He tells some people to teach school and witness for him through their contact with students. My friend who teaches first grade teaches her students how to talk to God. As she does this, her job seems bigger than that of a teacher who teaches students to read and write but does not teach them about God.

I was impressed with an article in *The Commission*, a foreign mission magazine put out by Southern Baptists. The story was told of a family who had saved their money to buy a motorboat for pleasure. They heard a missionary to Africa tell of how many more people he would be able to reach for Christ if only he had a boat. They talked and prayed about this need and decided God wanted them to give their boat to the missionary. The boat they had used for pleasure became more valuable. It began being used for a higher purpose.

I am reminded of the foreign missionary I invited to speak at a statewide teenage gathering. He was Glen Grobe, who witnessed up and down three hundred miles of the Amazon River Valley. He told of many adventures. Once he and a fellow missionary were on a journey in the boat when the tide was low, and they were unable to operate the boat. They did not know when the water level would rise enough so they could journey to the nearest shore. Their food and water might run out.

They were faced with the decision whether to wait and see or to get out and push and pull the boat. Stepping into the water was dangerous because the Amazon was known to contain man-eating fish. These small fish could, by the hundreds, attack a man and eat off all his flesh in a short time. Glen said he voted to push the boat. His fellow missionary voted to stay inside the boat. Glen wound up pushing and pulling his co-worker inside the boat. By God's protection and goodness, he made it to shore safely. He was a fisher of men, we can be sure. God called Glen to follow him to Brazil and to many adventures.

I once took a student home with me for several days. It was the close of school, and I was her counselor. Because of conflicts with her parents, she had nowhere to go. At night she would withdraw to her room. I discovered she was worrying about her boyfriend who had serious emotional problems and upsets.

I began going in each night to have a devotional time with Ann. I would read some encouraging Bible truth, and I would pray out loud for her and her boyfriend. I would ask God to help John with his problems and lead them concerning their future.

The fall came, and John and Ann both returned to school. John continued to have many problems. I talked hours with Ann and John about their fears and upsets. I sometimes asked them if they would mind if I prayed out loud for them. They would say it was all right. I believe it helps us to hear others pray for us. When people feel weak, I think such an experience can help them believe more in God's power and begin to look to him for help.

One day Ann told me John had come to her upset. She said she did not know what to do. She was surprised to hear herself tell John she was going to pray for him. She said the words came out easily.

I believe my job is not just to be a Christian counselor. Serving Christ makes my job bigger and more important.

Will you let God lead you as you seek his job for you in the future?

Devotional for Children 3: A Leader and a Teacher

Read Matthew 10:1-6; 11:1.

All of us are teachers and leaders to somebody. Jesus taught caring for others. He led his followers to heal, to teach about God, to get power over evil through prayer. When people follow you, what do they do? When people learn from you, what do you teach them?

One year my friend who teaches first grade taught a bright little girl who came from a home where she received proper care. She was taught good manners. She was happy and loving in her attitude. She never stole anything or told lies. One day, however, she told her teacher about going to the zoo with her family. She said, "My father told them I was younger than I am, so I could get in free." This dishonest act had made a strong impression.

Do you teach people to trust you or to mistrust you? I was teaching a Sunday School class at my church. It was for young people in the eleventh and twelfth grades at school. One day one of the young men in the class told about how he would promise to do things and then not show up if something better came along. A girl friend spoke up and said, "Oh, is that what happened the many times you said you would come to my house on Sunday night and didn't come?" He laughed nervously.

In our class that day we talked about how important it is to be "a person of our word." In other words, I teach you to trust me if I do what I say I will do. I teach you not to believe me if I do not do what I say I will do. For Jesus to teach the truth about God, he had to teach people they could count on him. To do this, he had to be honest.

Jesus said God loved us. He showed us how much God loved us by giving up his life on the cross. Because Jesus showed men how to love, those who follow him do many loving things for others.

I have a friend who loves God. She has not so much told me as she has shown me. She goes to see sick people much of the time. She collected money to help send the son of missionaries on a trip to visit his parents. The son was studying in the United States. His parents were in Peru. You can imagine how homesick he was. She helped him spend the summer with his parents because she loves God.

My friend opens her home to others. A young Korean woman married an American serviceman. After they came to the United States, he began being cruel to her. They have one child. My friend has let this Korean woman stay with her some and has been a good friend to her. She took her to church to try to help her know God.

Do you ever complain that your parents will not let you do things you want to do? Maybe you have taught them that you are careless and lazy by your behavior at home. If your job is to feed the dog and walk him every day, do you do this or do you have to be reminded and then complain? Do your parents find you watching TV when they have told you to study? Do you tell them you are going one place but you go somewhere else?

If you are dishonest and do not carry out your chores at home, you teach your parents to question how grown up you are. Then, when you ask for certain privileges, they may say no.

Once a boy at my school needed some medicine. He begged me to take him. I was busy, but wanted to help. We stopped at K-Mart to get the prescription filled as we came from the doctor. I waited and waited. The boy, Joe, was gone for the prescription about forty-five minutes. Finally, I went in and saw no line at the prescription counter. I found Joe and asked about the long delay. He made up a story about the pharmacist having to go to a building behind the store to get his medicine.

I said nothing. As I thought the matter over, I realized there was no building behind K-Mart. I knew Joe had been dishonest. He had talked to me earlier about people letting him down. He said he was glad he could see I cared about him. He said he trusted me and felt I was like a mother to him.

I sought Joe after school and said to him: "Joe, you have talked a lot about trust since we have been friends. I went out of my way personally to take you to your doctor today. You were dishonest with me. There is no building where the pharmacist could have gone for medicine. I expect you to be as honest with me as I am with you. Don't be unfair with me again." He promised he would be honest from then on.

Jesus always led people in the right direction. Our goal should be the same as his.

Devotional for Children 4: The Bad Becomes Good

Read Acts 16. Give special attention to verses 16-40.

Paul and Silas were on their famous missionary journey that included a vision from God. A man of Greece called them to come and begin a witness on the continent of Europe. They met a group of women praying together beside a river. One of the women was Lydia, a merchant who sold purple cloth. Although Lydia was a believer, Paul was able to give her greater understanding. She and her household were baptized by Paul. Both Paul and Silas were then invited to be guests in her home.

Paul and Silas met a demon-possessed slave girl who was a fortune teller. Her masters earned lots of money from her ability. To rid the girl of the demon, Paul commanded it out of her in the name of Jesus. Her masters were angry because they could no longer use her to make money. They grabbed Paul and Silas and yelled, "These Jews are ruining our city. They are teaching the people to do things that are against the Roman laws."

A mob was then formed against Paul and Silas. The judges ordered them stripped and beaten with wooden whips. Afterwards they were thrown into prison. The jailer was threatened with death if they escaped, so he put them in the dungeon and clamped their feet into the stocks.

Most people would be very upset over such a bad situation, but Paul and Silas were praying and singing in their cell about midnight. Suddenly an earthquake shook all the chains off the prisoners and the doors swung open. The jailer thought the prisoners had escaped and started to kill himself with a sword. Paul and Silas called to him not to harm himself, saying that they were still there.

After this shocking experience, the jailer was ready to hear the gospel. He asked how to be saved. Not only did he accept Christ as Savior, but he invited Paul and Silas into his home. Soon his family also became Christians. The jailer washed their stripes and fed them.

Sometimes what looks like a bad situation can be turned into a good one. What matters is our attitude and our actions. Paul and Silas could have pouted and complained.

17
Emotionalism and Decision Time

For teenagers attending camp for as long as seven days or more, perhaps decision services might be constructive. But for children younger than thirteen, I would suggest any decision to accept Christ as personal Savior, to rededicate themselves to Christ, or to commit themselves to some special calling should be made known to a counselor or other staffer. At times campers should be encouraged to talk to the camp director, minister, or missionary. Public decisions can then be made at their home church.

One observation I made about the campers who were nine to twelve years of age was how easily they were influenced. If campers began to go down the aisle to make decisions, the children seemed clear about what this meant. They often told the minister or me they wanted to accept Christ as personal Savior or to live a better Christian life when they went home. In other instances, campers would be vague. They obviously feared being left out of something a friend was doing, or of entering into what seemed most acceptable behavior.

Decision time sometimes became emotional. This deeply concerned me. I came to urge our camp pastors to make their statement of invitation quite brief. I stressed that they be clear and very unemotional. Sometimes this directive seemed difficult to follow. Other times I saw a pastor do exactly as I suggested and still saw many girls begin crying. Once one camper cried, others chimed in until we were flooded with emotion.

Once two campers had continued to disrupt their cabin when they went to prepare for bed. I went to the cabin to settle them. I asked the two campers who were bawling to follow me to my office. When we arrived, I said to one child, "What are you crying about?"

She said, "My brother died."

I said, "I'm sorry. When did this happen?"

"Five years ago," she sobbed.

Looking at the other camper, I asked, "And what are you crying about?"

"Her brother died," she answered between sobs.

I promptly told the children that they had cried quite enough for one evening and that the brother was with God. I said I wanted them to stop crying and settle down to go to bed. They seemed to need that admonition, and they promptly did as I requested.

For us to have service in the chapel with some 180-200 campers nine to twelve years of age was an unnatural setting. We had some forty to fifty staffers and guests scattered among them. But in their churches there would be a mixture of men and women, older teenagers, elderly folks, and the like, scattered among and between nine- to twelve-year-old children. Therefore, it would not be as easily an emotional setting as we had.

I believe staff members should be carefully selected for their ability to be calm amid any form of chaos among children. If a staff member acts anxious, whether about a bloody nose or about concern over parents who have not accepted Christ, campers will easily lose their "cool." I observed that our campers nine to twelve could become hysterical with slight provocation.

We had a camper to say she saw her dead grandmother walking through the prayer garden after lights out at night. It took the counselor a while to settle her cabin after this upset. A flying squirrel that got into a cabin one night set two or three cabins astir. A small fire started in the kitchen and awoke the entire camp as the alarm spread. One camper fainted and others cried. I needed a calm and stable staff to reassure campers.

Emotionalism is not uncommon when children are

in large numbers and away from home. We had sudden summer storms. The lights sometimes went out momentarily, and this always resulted in screams from younger children. At times a bat would fly out of the chapel gable during a candlelight service. This produced everything but a worship experience. The staffers who served during those times still enjoy retelling "bat" stories.

Time to go to bed was a critical time for the homesick. It was also a time for making up excuses to stay up past time for lights-out. The counselor who kept staying up at night to talk to some camper with a problem only made the problem worse. Children need adequate rest. Without this rest, everything becomes more critical. Staffers also need adequate rest. If they do not get it, their nerves will be on edge.

Decision time at camp was only one opportunity for an outbreak of emotionalism, but it could possibly result in more emotionally damaging experiences than most others.

Surely children need God presented as a God of love. No person should be invited to speak to children who presents God as someone they should fear.

I would strongly oppose services for youth where messages stress the sinfulness of dancing, smoking, and going to movies and discos. Messages about God's nature, the call to service, and the joy of Christian fellowship are more appropriate. Inspiration can be drawn from the lives of famous Christians: Albert Schweitzer, Martin Luther, Jane Addams, and many others.

18
Closing Challenge

I see the challenge of camping as a call to create an atmosphere of caring and acceptance. Every week I talk with young people who have felt rejection so often that they struggle to find enough confidence to face the simplest demands of life.

Today a boy said to me, "Miss Sanders, you must be sick of talking to me about my problems. I know you must think I am dumb to act the way I do."

I told him to stop projecting onto me these negative attitudes toward himself that are not accurate. I told him I see him as an attractive person, that I genuinely like him, that I am perfectly willing to give him the time necessary to help him learn to be a winner. I said that I do feel deeply concerned when I hear that he has broken some rule and gotten into trouble.

When he told me that he had gone into the girls' dorm, which was against the rules, he excused himself by saying that he *felt* he did not do anything wrong. I confronted him with the fallacy in his thinking. There are rules to abide by in a job, at home, at school. He broke a rule which is wrong and has its penalty. Much of the rejection he has faced has been a result of breaking the rules of his family and his former school. Until he faces life's basic demands, he will continue to fail and to be rejected.

I am trying to acquaint him with the willful Child personality that lives inside him. This Child has had *his way* too long. When Mike listens to his Child, he is led by his *feelings*. He makes poor decisions. I am continually plugging into the Adult ego state in Mike that reasons, thinks, plans, and can help him become a winner. I accept and care for Mike, but I reject his self-defeating behavior.

Many campers will come to camp who need relationships that show respect and that challenge the best that is in them. The prevalence of broken homes is creating many complex situations: several sets of children in one family with competitiveness at new levels, a boyfriend living with the mother, and shuffling back and forth of children between mother and father who are now married to somebody else. Increasing use of alcohol and drugs at home and school is creating life-styles that place added pressure on all who are involved.

Dr. William Glasser, famous psychiatrist and creator of the Reality Therapy approach in counseling, says that we have two very basic needs: (1) to love and be loved, and (2) to involve ourselves in some meaningful work or project that gives us a sense of worth. He says that we can get the love need met through one relationship of adequate emotional involvement but that ideally we need many relationships and interactions to sustain life at a satisfying level. Research has indicated that the person who has adequate friends and loved ones with whom he is often interacting seems less likely to get physically sick than the person who is more alone.

Research on touching indicates that adequate touching is necessary for persons to be physically and emotionally healthy. Some studies indicate that people who have pets such as dogs and cats tend to be healthier because they touch the animals. The animals like to sit on their laps or lie close to them.

I wonder how much of the promiscuity among young people is actually due to their lack of physical warmth from family and friends. We all need touching that has nothing to do with sex to feel secure and accepted.

One loving relationship can make an impact on a camper, even in one week. The movie *On Golden Pond* is about an eighty-year-old man and a thirteen-year-old boy who establish adequate emotional involvement through fishing, boating, and sharing adventure together. They both emerge with a new sense of worth and inner fulfillment. If camping can do this for any two people, it will be worth all our efforts.

The sense of worth comes to people in different ways. I have a friend who has always wanted to be a nurse. After her junior year in college, she began working for an orthopedic surgeon. He values her skill, and her times of sharing with us express enthusiasm and challenge.

A student I know has always had difficulty in learning. However, in our school she has become a dorm counselor, has carried out her duties well, and has gained the confidence of students and staff.

Young people attending camp need experiences of participation that create a sense of worth. They need to be helped to see and appreciate their talents and be willing to be led into some worthwhile ministry in the future.

The challenge to be faced in *Christian* camping is a challenge to guide young people in establishing some personal values that will give direction to life.

By Supreme Court ruling religion has been mostly ruled out of the schools. Homes are so unstable that it is often evident that little teaching of values is done at home. Young people have sometimes been urged to get all the education they can, but they lack meaning and direction to the point that they do not know what to do with the training they get. I believe the lack of values has greatly contributed to the statistics that report the suicide rate among American young people as the highest it has ever been.

The camp that can help young people clarify for themselves some meaningful values will be the camp that gives hope and purpose to youth who can make this a better world in which to live. I purposely talk about "helping clarify values" because I do not believe the best approach is to seek to superimpose your values upon the belief system of another person.

It seems that teaching people to question themselves, to look at the basic truths of the Bible, and to project how they can live out their faith in daily life can make a profound contribution to some persons.

Presenting Jesus Christ as a living person who can love and guide can do more for people than merely teaching principles. Those who wish to make him known need to experience him personally and to continually study the Gospels to be true to his character.

If you direct a camp where a few young people experience a new way of caring that accepts them but also confronts them with life's true demands, then you are succeeding. If you direct a camp where youth begin to feel they are valuable and that they can become involved in making this a better world, then you are succeeding. If you help just one young person to know and love Christ, and that love gives meaning and direction, then you are succeeding.

Bibliography

CHAPTER 2—PRAYER IN CAMP PROGRAMMING
Rinker, Rosalind. *Prayer: Conversing with God* (Grand Rapids, Mich.: Zondervan Publishing House, 1959). Conversational prayer explained.

CHAPTER 3—BIBLE STUDY IN CAMP
Carkhuff, Robert R. *Helping and Human Relations* (New York: Holt, Rinehart and Winston, Inc., 1969). The clarifying response explained.

CHAPTER 4—A BIBLE STUDY: GROWING
IN CHRISTIAN DISCIPLESHIP
Alberti, Robert E., Emmons, Michael L. *Your Perfect Right* (San Luis Obispo, Calif.: Impact, 1974). Assertiveness explained.

Boom, Corrie ten. *Tramp for the Lord* (Old Tappan, N.J.: Fleming H. Revell Company, 1974).

Frankl, Viktor E. *Man's Search for Meaning* (New York: Washington Press Square, Inc., 1963).

Fredericks, Carlton. *Breast Cancer: A Nutritional Approach* (New York: Grosset & Dunlap Publishers, 1977). Reference to low sugar and low salt diet.

Glasser, William. *Positive Addiction* (New York: Harper & Row Publishers, 1976).

Marshall, Catherine. *The Helper* (New York: Avon Books, 1978).

Redhead, John A. *Letting God Help You* (New York: Abingdon Press, 1967).

Wilkerson, David. *Run, Baby, Run* (New York: Jove Publications, 1969). Reference to Nicky Cruz.

Worchester, J. H., Jr. *David Livingstone* (Evanston, Ill.: Moody Press, 1980).

CHAPTER 6—USING BEHAVIOR MODIFICATION
TO SHAPE BEHAVIOR
Becker, Wesley C.; Engelmann, Siegfried; Thomas, Don R. *Teaching a Course in Applied Psychology* (Chicago: Science Research Associates, 1971). Reference to behavior modification.

CHAPTER 7—HOW OUR PERSONALITY STATES AFFECT
RELATIONSHIPS
Harris, Thomas A. *I'm OK—You're OK* (New York: Harper & Row, Publishers, 1969). Reference to Transactional Analysis.

James, Muriel and Jongeward, Dorothy. *Born to Win* (Reading, Mass.: Addison-Wesley Publishing Company, 1971). Reference to Transactional Analysis, Parent, Adult, Child.

Powell, John. *Why Am I Afraid to Tell You Who I Am?* (Niles, Ill.: Argus Communications, 1969). Reference to Transactional Analysis.

CHAPTER 8—BREAKING UP PSYCHOLOGICAL GAMES
Berne, Eric. *Games People Play* (New York: Random House, Inc., 1964).

Ernst, Kenneth. *Games Students Play* (Millbrae, Calif.: Celestial Arts Publishing, 1972).

CHAPTER 13—DRAMAS
Andrew, Brother, et al. *God's Smuggler* (Carmel, N.Y.: Guideposts Associates, Inc., 1967). Reference made in "Hold Out Your Light."

Bainton, Roland. *Here I Stand* (New York: Abingdon Press, 1951). Reference to Martin Luther in "Hold Out Your Light."

Bolton, Sarah K. *Lives of Girls Who Became Famous* (New York: Thomas Y. Crowell Company, rev. ed. 1949). Reference to Marian Anderson, Florence Nightingale in "Hold Out Your Light."

Bowie, Walter Russell. *Women of Light* (New York: Harper & Row Publishers, 1964). Reference to Susanna Wesley, Florence Nightingale in "Hold Out Your Light."

Bueltmann, A. J. *White Queen of the Cannibals* (Evanston, Ill.: Moody Press, 1956). Reference to Mary Slessor in "Hold Out Your Light."

Deen, Edith. *Great Women of the Christian Faith* (New York: Harper & Row, Publishers, 1959). Reference to Susanna Wesley, Florence Nightingale, Mary Slessor in "Hold Out Your Light."

Fletcher, Jesse T. *Bill Wallace of China* (Nashville, Tenn.: Broadman Press, 1963). See "Hold Out Your Light."

Gibran, Kahlil. *The Prophet* (New York: Alfred Knopf, 1960). Quotation concerning children in "Stable Bows and Living Arrows."

Hussong, Clara. *The Golden Picture Book of Birds* (New

York: Golden Press, 1959). Reference to characteristics of these birds: woodpeckers, mockingbirds, mourning doves, killdeer in play "More Valuable than Birds."

Lemmon, Robert S. *Our Amazing Birds* (Garden City, N.Y.: American Garden Guild and Doubleday & Company, Inc., 1952). Reference to characteristics of these birds: cedar waxwings, scarlet tanager, mockingbird, cowbird in the play "More Valuable than Birds."

Mersand, Joseph. *Great American Short Biographies* (New York: Dell Publishing Co., Inc., 1966). Reference to Marian Anderson in the play "Hold Out Your Light."

Peale, Norman Vincent. *Sin, Sex, and Self-Control* (New York: Fawcett Book Group, 1977). Reference to sex in play called "Conflict."

Wilson, Dorothy Clark. *Dr. Ida* (New York: Friendship Press, 1976). Reference to Dr. Ida Scudder of India in the play "Hold Out Your Light."

Chapter 16—Use of Devotional Thoughts

Andrew, Brother, et al. *God's Smuggler* (Carmel, N.Y.: Guideposts Associates, Inc., 1967). Reference to Brother Andrew in Staffer Devotional 1.

Bainton, Roland. *Here I Stand* (New York: Abingdon Press, 1950). Reference to Martin Luther in Teenage Devotional 2.

Miller, Madeline S., Miller, J. Lane. *Harper's Bible Dictionary* (New York: Harper & Row Publishers, 1961).

Redhead, John A. *Letting God Help You* (New York: Abingdon Press, 1967). Reference to mind as barrel in Teenage Devotional 1.

Sherrill, Lewis. *The Struggle of the Soul* (New York: The Macmillan Company, 1951). Reference to life as a treadmill, saga, pilgrimage in Staffer Devotional 1.

Weatherhead, Leslie D. *In Quest of a Kingdom* (New York: Abingdon Press, 1944). Reference to interpretation of the prodigal son in Staffer Devotional 4.

Weatherhead, Leslie D. *Wounded Spirits* (New York: Abingdon Press, 1963). Reference to sleepwalker concerns the case of Monica Cowling in Teenage Devotional 1.

Chapter 18—Closing Challenge

Glasser, William. *Reality Therapy* (New York: Harper & Row, 1965). Reference to our basic emotional needs.

Glasser, William. *The Identity Society* (New York: Harper & Row, Publishers, 1972).

Montague, Ashley. *Touching* (New York: Harper & Row, Publishers, 1976). Reference to touch and its effect on mental health.